Olde St. John's

STORIES FROM A SEAPORT CITY

Olde St. John's

STORIES FROM A SEAPORT CITY

Best Wishes!
Frank Galgay
&
Mike McCarthy

Frank Galgay

&

Michael McCarthy

Flanker Press Ltd.
St. John's, Newfoundland
2001

Flanker Press Ltd.
P O Box 2522, Stn C, St. John's
Newfoundland, Canada, A1C 6K1

Toll Free: 1-866-739-4420
Telephone: (709) 739-4477
Facsimile: (709) 739-4420
E-mail: info@flankerpress.com
Web site: www.flankerpress.com

National Library of Canada Cataloguing in Publication Data

Galgay, Frank, 1940-
Olde St. John's : stories from a seaport city

Includes bibliographical references and index.
ISBN 1-894463-15-3

1. St. John's (Nfld.)—History. I. McCarthy, Michael J., 1932- II. Title.

FC2196.4.G34 2001 971.8'1 C2001-903664-7
F1124.5.S14G34 2001

Second printing May 2002
Printed in Canada by Robinson-Blackmore
St. John's, Newfoundland, Canada.

Dedication

This book is dedicated to the memory of former mayor Andrew Greene Carnell, and former mayor and councillor Dorothy Wyatt.

Mayor Carnell served St. John's well during his four consecutive terms of office. During this time he did much to help improve the living conditions of the citizens of St. John's by introducing the first city bus line and setting up a commission of inquiry to look into the deplorable housing conditions that existed in St. John's. This resulted in the setting up of the Newfoundland and Labrador Housing Agency.

Andrew G. Carnell

During the early days of the appointed Commission of Government that ruled Newfoundland from 1934 to 1949, Mayor Carnell led the only democratically elected government in Newfoundland. He was famous for his wit and greatly feared by the commissioners who were not used to being mocked in public for their pomposity. They feared Mayor Carnell because he was not shy in proclaiming the need for an elected government. He died on January 26, 1951.

Dorothy Wyatt

Mayor Dorothy Wyatt was the first woman elected to council and the first female mayor of St. John's. During her twenty-eight years of service, Dorothy Wyatt was true to her slogan, "Wyatt won't be quiet." She won the hearts of the citizens of St. John's and became a legend in her own time. Mrs. Wyatt passed away on September 23, 2001 and was the first person ever to be elected posthumously to St. John's City Council, on September 25, 2001.

Acknowledgements

Dr. Gerald Benson
Cal Best and staff of the Provincial Archives
Geoffrey Carnell, Jr.
Burnham Gill
Captain Tom Goodyear
David Leamon and staff of the Provincial Reference Library
Jack Martin
Helen Miller, City of St. John's Archives
Captain Joe Prim

Cover:
The former Rendell-Shea residence at 82 Cochrane Street
presently owned by Bruce and Jane Blackwood.
Photo by Garry Cranford.

Table of Contents

SECTION I 1
Introduction to the Historic City of St. John's

SECTION II 35
Women in Eighteenth Century St. John's

SECTION III 49
Crime and Punishment in Eighteenth Century St. John's

SECTION IV 65
Flaming History: Fires in St. John's

SECTION V 83
Shipwrecks In and Around St. John's

SECTION VI 107
The Ghosts and Haunted Places of St. John's

SECTION VII 125
Highlights of the Mayors of St. John's

APPENDICES
A: City Council Members 1888-1997 155
B: Partial List of Shipwrecks Near St. John's 175
C: Interesting Events in St. John's History 179
D: Letters from St. John's 188
E: Names of Subscribers
to the Royal Newfoundland Gazette in 1807 197
F: List of Crew and Passengers
Coming to St. John's on the Liven in 1815 200

Bibliography 203
Index 207

Section I

Introduction to the Historic City of St. John's

WATER STREET AROUND 1890. (ST. JOHN'S CITY ARCHIVES)

First Account of Fishermen Using St. John's

The city of St. John's can trace its roots back to the early sixteenth century. The earliest reference to the city is in a letter by John Rut, dated St. John's Harbour, August 3, 1527. In this letter, Rut reported to King Henry VIII of England that there were fourteen ships, none of them English, in St. John's Harbour. In 1542, St. John's was chosen as the place of rendezvous for Jacques Cartier and the Sieur de Roberval. They reported seventeen French ships in St. John's.

*Sir Humphrey Gilbert reading his commission on the site of the St. John's War Memorial August 5, 1583. (*The Story of Newfoundland, *Cochrane & Parsons)*

On August 3, 1583, Sir Humphrey Gilbert entered St. John's Harbour with three ships, and a few days later took possession of Newfoundland for the Queen of England. He reported thirty-six ships in the harbour, sixteen of which were English. The other twenty ships were Portuguese and Spanish. Gilbert reported that the English were now the acknowledged masters of St. John's Harbour. He also reported houses and a place called the "Garden," where the merchants took their walks. Before leaving, Gilbert gave title to a number of English merchants for their fishing premises in St. John's Harbour.

Pirates in St. John's

In 1596, a French pirate, Michel de Sance, pillaged the English ships in St. John's Harbour. In 1614, Sir Richard Whitbourne met the English privateer Sir Henry Mainwaring, who arrived at St. John's with five ships. Whitbourne described St. John's as a good harbour for ships and fishing.

The St. John's Plantation

In 1613, the population of St. John's was listed as sixty-two. In 1628, W. Payne described St. John's as "the prime and chief lot in the country." He referred to some houses having already been built there.

Seventeenth century Newfoundland fishing stage. (National Archives of Canada)

Kirke Fortifies St. John's and The Dutch Raid

In 1638, Sir David Kirke fortified St. John's by erecting a number of cannons to guard the harbour. However, by 1665, Kirke's cannons had disappeared and St. John's was pillaged by the Dutch raider de Ruyter. De Ruyter said later that six cannons would have prevented him from entering St. John's Harbour.

The First Official Census (1675)

The first official census of the resident English planters in St. John's was made in 1675 by Sir John Berry. The permanent residents together with their children and servants were listed.

Sir John Berry's Census of St. John's, 1675 (original spelling)

Planters	Sons	Daughters	Men	Boats	Stages	Trainfats
Jno. Downing & Wife	0	3	31	31	2	1
Wm. Bennet & Wife	1	0	15	3	1	1
Tho. Oxford & Wife	4	4	21	4	1	1
Denice Loney & Wife	0	1	16	4	2	2
Phillip Roberts & wife	2	0	9	2	1	1
James Even & Wife	4	0	2	1	1	1
Thomas Dodd & Wife	1	3	9	2	1	1
Mary Frize (Widow)	2	3	18	4	2	2
Andrew Oxon & Wife	0	0	15	3	1	1
George Peircey	0	0	3	1	1	0
Jno. Hollowell & Wife	2	2	5	2	1	0
Wm. Caines & Wife	0	0	3	1	1	1

Richard Hopkins & Wife	0	0	5	1	1	1
Wm. Matthews & wife	0	2	9	2	1	0
Tho. Holloways	1	1	9	2	1	1
Jno. Collins	0	1	6	2	1	1
Jno. Hood & Wife	2	1	2	2	1	1
Richard England	0	0	6	2	1	0
Jno. Piercey	0	0	5	2	1	1

155 cattle + some sheep

St. John's around 1770. (Drawing belonging to Governor Edwards—reproduced from Prowse's *History of Newfoundland*)

Orders to Remove Illegally Built Houses and Sheds

The growth of the St. John's population was greatly hindered by the naval commander's orders to remove houses and stages erected without permission. In 1711, Commander Josias Crowe ordered the following to remove their buildings:

> That the Tenements, Store Houses & Stages now in possession of the persons undermentioned (to wit) Richard Colesworthy Upper Stage, House and room at the fort at Bursthart Hill, Captain Stafford in behalf of Henry Perden, one storehouse on the Vice-

Admiral's Room, Thomas and John Squarry, one storehouse on the Admiral's Room, Mr. Tuffs on behalf of Mrs. Ann Earll the upper stage adjoining to his own two boats room, Governor Collins in behalf of Mr. Holeman, one storehouse on the Vice-Admiral's Room. Hugh Trencher in behalf of John Harris Esq. of Exon, one storehouse on the Admiral's Room. Captain Holesworthy in behalf of Richard Martin, one storehouse on the Admiral's Room Being proved formally belonging to fishing ships & ingrosed since the year 1665 contrary to Act of Parliament to the prejudice of the said ships. I do hereby dispossess them of the same in the right of the fishing ships for the next season and they are accordingly dispossessed.

The Fortification of St. John's

In 1688, the British Government gave 3,000 pounds to fortify St. John's, and Fort William was built and manned by British soldiers. In 1697, Colonel John Gibsone reported to the Lords of the Council of Trade on the state of St. John's following an attack by the French:

> We arrived here in St. John's on June 7 (1697). On our arrival here we found nothing but destruction and ruin, not a house standing, but one, and but four families upon the place, but several have come since from Placentia. The want of materials on our first arrival has been very prejudicial to us, for we could neither command, spade, shovel or pickax, that it was with very much ado, that we could with the help of the Grenadiers' Hatchet make huts to shelter our soldiers from the weather, but now the store ships being come, all hands shall be put to work.

While they were building the new fortifications, the French navy appeared but did not attack when they found a number of English men-of-war, all in line, broadside to the mouth of the harbour. At the end of his letter, Colonel Gibsone reported that he had left St. John's fortified with two redoubts, one of nine guns on the south side and one of five guns on the north. There was also a fort a little within the harbour. The batteries at the harbour mouth were finished, but not the fort in the harbour. As well, he left twelve officers and two hundred and twenty soldiers to guard the town under the command of Major Thomas Handside.

The Southside Castle

Around 1701, a strong fort known as the "Castle" was built on the Southside. In 1703, a boom was placed across the mouth of the Narrows as part of the town's defences. In 1773, a new fort was constructed on an eminence overlooking the Narrows and was first called the Grand Battery. This new fort was large enough to garrison about 500 soldiers. In 1779, the fort was renamed Fort Townshend. It also became the official residence of the Newfoundland Governors from 1781 until Government House was built in 1831. In 1867, Britain withdrew the Fort Townshend garrison, the ramparts were demolished, and most of the buildings were abandoned. The site then became the headquarters of the Newfoundland police force. The old barracks were demolished in 1947. The Fort Townshend site is now the proposed site for a new provincial museum, archives and art gallery, to be called The Rooms.

St. John's in 1789. Fort Townshend on the skyline. (From a water colour drawing by R. P. Brenton in the British Museum. Outline of Newfoundland History, *L. E. F. English)*

French Attacks on St. John's

Between 1696 and 1709, St. John's was attacked three times and pillaged by a mixed army of Canadian Indians, regular French soldiers, and settlers from Placentia. In the winter of 1708-09, the citizens of St. John's had to pay seven thousand two hundred eighty pounds to ransom their property from St. Ovide, who commanded the attacking French force. The following year John Collins was elected commandant of St. John's and the area from St. John's to Ferryland and on to Carbonear Island.

A French artist's picture of a French attack on St. John's in the early eighteenth century. (Public Archives of Canada)

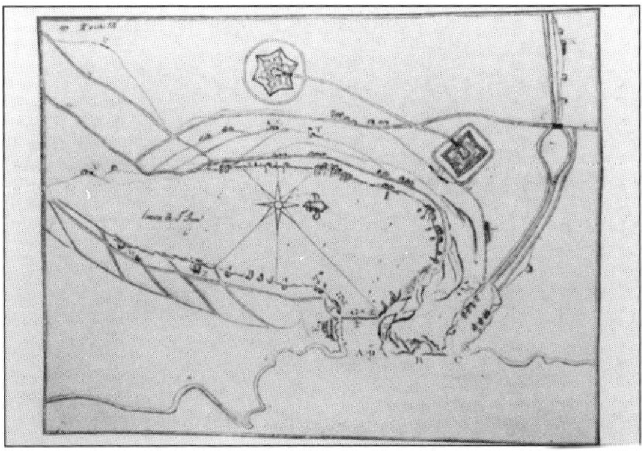

Sketch of St. John's Harbour in 1779. Sketch was made from memory by the captain of a French privateer who had spent four months as a prisoner of war in St. John's. (Public Archives of Canada)

In 1762, St. John's was again captured by the French, who landed at Bay Bulls and came overland. The town was taken on June 27, 1762 and they remained in control until September 20, when the British landed at Torbay and after a sharp battle for Signal Hill recaptured the town. In 1796, a French fleet appeared off St. John's. The town was put under martial law, but the French ships made no attempt to enter the Narrows. They did capture and burn Bay Bulls.

View of the Narrows, St. John's around 1800. (*The Story of Newfoundland*, Cochrane & Parsons)

First Local St. John's Militia

From 1709 to 1740, there were no repairs to the fortifications at St. John's, and no soldiers were stationed there. In 1741, the citizens of St. John's formed a local militia, repaired the old forts and were given ten cannons to defend their town. Soldiers were again stationed in St. John's after 1740 and remained at St. John's until 1867.

Appointment of First Governor of Newfoundland

In 1729, Captain Henry Osborne RN was appointed Governor of Newfoundland, and he ruled the island from his warship anchored in St. John's Harbour. He appointed Keen, Weston and Southmead as the first St. John's magistrates. In 1730, he had a courthouse and prison built at St. John's. This, together with the Governor residing in Newfoundland all year long, was the first indication that St. John's had become the seat of government for the island.

First Police Force in St. John's

Until the appointment of Captain Osborne as Governor of Newfoundland, law enforcement was under the control of the fishing admiral of the port. In 1729, Governor Osborne appointed four justices and four constables to maintain law and order in St. John's. At one time, tavern owners had to act as constables as part of getting their license; this included women who operated taverns. Later, they paid a sum of money instead to hire constables. In 1871, the Newfoundland Constabulary was established, which later became the Royal Newfoundland Constabulary.

St. John's Fire Department

As early as 1711, St. John's had fire patrols. In 1811, the Merchants' Society organized the first formal fire brigade for St. John's. In 1833, the newly elected Newfoundland Legislature reorganized the St. John's Fire Companies. In 1888, firefighting in St. John's came under the control of the municipal government. In 1895, the fire department was placed under the Superintendent of Police, and this arrangement continued until 1957, when the St. John's Fire Department was placed under the provincial Department of Justice.

St. John's Harbour in March, 1838 with sealing fleet going through the St. John's Narrows. (*Outline of Newfoundland History*, L. E. F. English. Reproduction of John Robertson collection)

The Coming of the Irish to St. John's

There had been a trickle of Irish immigrants coming to Newfoundland before the end of the seventeenth century. In

1750, Governor Drake reported 600 Irish in St. John's. A census three years later shows that there were 669 Irish-born and 454 English-born inhabitants in the general St. John's area. In 1766, Reverend Edward Langman reported that more Irish men had come to St. John's from Waterford than in the past fourteen years. The next year, Governor Hugh Palliser ordered that the "huts" erected by the Irish in St. John's were to be pulled down and no more were to be erected.

However, the Irish immigrants continued to arrive in great numbers, and by 1790, of the 3,000 residents in St. John's, seventy per cent were Irish. Between 1798 and 1820, thousands of Irish immigrants settled in St. John's, swelling the population to over 10,000 residents. Some continued to come to Newfoundland after the 1820s, but they came in small numbers. On September 8, 1863, sixty-two stowaways landed from the Galway steamer *Adriatic*.

The Planned Irish Uprising of 1800

In the spring of 1800, Irish soldiers stationed at the St. John's forts planned to revolt and set up a Republic of

Customs House—Water Street and Kings Beach circa 1880. (St. John's City Archives)

Newfoundland. Thanks to Bishop O'Donel, the first Roman Catholic bishop of St. John's, the plot was discovered and put down. Five were put to death by the Powder Shed (now Belvedere Street), where a plaque marks the spot of the execution. The other mutineers were sent to Halifax, and three of them were executed there.

Formation of the Benevolent Irish Society

In 1806, a number of both Protestant- and Roman Catholic–born Irishmen met at the London Tavern in St. John's and founded the non-denominational Benevolent Irish Society. It is still in existence today, although in the summer of 1998 the B.I.S. building was sold and the Society moved to new quarters on Harvey Road.

For many years, the parade of the members of the Benevolent Irish Society on St. Patrick's Day was a great event. One early writer gave this description of the parade:

The London Tavern, where the non-denominational Benevolent Irish Society was founded in 1806. (B.I.S. Centenary Book, 1906)

> The Benevolent Irish Society, the oldest in our Island, paraded each St. Patrick's Day with colours flying, the officers bearing staffs in their hands, accompanied by three brass bands. The Society left the Irish Hall, and proceeded alternately, to last Mass at the Roman Catholic Cathederal (Basilica) and St. Patrick's church.
>
> After Mass they marched through the principal streets. The bands: Bennett's, The Total Abstinence Society and Star of the Sea, playing lively Irish airs. When one Band ceased, another began and when this finished the third took it up, thus keeping the music going all the time."

Construction of Cabot Tower in 1897. (St. John's City Archives)

Visit of Smith O'Brien, Irish Patriot

In 1859, Smith O'Brien, an Irish patriot, visited St. John's and spoke to a crowd of about 10,000 from the Basilica steps. He said he saw some informers from the past among the crowd.

On April 26, 1866, another famous Irishman, James Stephens, the head of the Fenians, arrived in St. John's, en route to New York. There was a $5,000 reward offered by the British Government for information leading to his capture, but he escaped detection and reached New York safely. Only four men knew of his arrival in St. John's, and only one man saw him.

In 1918, Prime Minister Sir Edward Patrick Morris, a St. John's native and son of an Irish immigrant, was raised to the British peerage as Baron Morris of Waterford.

View of St. John's around 1900. (*Guide to Newfoundland*, 1905)

Popular Leisure Pastimes in Nineteenth Century St. John's

Card Games

The great indoor recreation of the early nineteenth century in St. John's was cards, and Forty-fives was the game the fishermen and sailors played on the wharves and boats, often for high stakes. However, Whist was the popular game of ladies and gentlemen. There is a story of a certain lady who dozed in church and woke from her snooze in the middle of the sermon. Hearing the clergyman's voice, which had been evident at a card game in her house the night before, she immediately called out, "Hearts are trumps." This announcement greatly amused the congregation.

Horse Racing

Horse racing was a popular outdoor sport in old St. John's, and there were racecourses at Flower Hill, Avalon Course and Mount Pearl.

A Description of St. John's in 1813

In 1813, Lieutenant Edward Chappell wrote:

> The capital of Newfoundland consists of one very narrow street extending entirely along one side of the port. The houses are principally built of wood; and there are very few handsome or even good-looking edifices in the place. This street stands upon very irregular ground and is not paved; therefore, in wet weather it is rendered almost impassable, by mud and filth. There are a great number of small public houses, but scarcely one tolerable inn. The London Tavern, however, has a good billiard room attached to it. Shops of all descriptions are very numerous; but most commodities are extravagantly dear, particularly meat, poultry and vegetables.

St. John's Harbour around 1905. (*Guide to Newfoundland*, 1905)

The Taverns and Inns in St. John's in 1807

Upper Division
(from Riverhead to Mr. Boucher's Farm)

Licensed to	Tavern Sign	Licensed to	Tavern Sign
William Best	**Bunch of Grapes**	John Hayse	**Ship**
John Widdicombe	**Rose and Crown**	Edward Angell	**Britannia**
John Williams	Name omitted	John Cahill	**Tavern for All Weather**

Patrick F Murine	**Flower Pot**	Will McCarthy	**Hope**
Rich. Heaney	**Struggler**	Mike Murphy	**Dove**
Mary Hennessey	**Royal Standard**		

Middle Division
(from Boucher's Farm to Job's Cove)

Pat. Resmond	**Ship Assistance**	Will Power	**Angel**
Angus Macnamara	**Agincourt**	Will Welsh	**Swan**
Roberty Dooling	**Red Cow**	John Fitzgerald	**Jolly Fisherman**
Edmund Doyle	**Blue Ball**	Mike Hanlon	**Shoulder Of Mutton**
Dominick King	**White Hart**	Graham Little	name omitted
Richard Perchard	**Royal Oak**	Margaret Walsh	**Sailor**

Lower Division
(from Job's Cove to eastermost part of St. John's)

Cornelius Quick	**London Tavern**	Robert Brien	**Butchery**
Dennis Murphy	**Wheatsheaf**	Dan Driscoll	**Bird In Hand**
Patrick Walsh	**Union Flag**	William Welsh	**?**
John Murphy	**Duke of York**	Mike Mara	**Sun**
Charles Power	**Plough**	Tom Murphy	**Three Crowns**

Land Permitted in St. John's

On June 26, 1813, Governor Keats requested people needing land to make application for land grants. Land sale was now legal.

The Early Churches of St. John's

The first place of worship in St. John's was a Church of England chapel built around 1699 "within the precincts of Fort William." The Anglican Cathedral was opened in the fall of 1850, and after being badly damaged in the 1892 fire, it was rebuilt.

The "Old Chapel," and "Old Palace," St. John's, built by Bishop O'Donel.

The "Old Chapel" and "Old Palace," St. John's, built by Bishop O'Donel. (B.I.S. Centenary Book, 1906)

In 1799, the first Roman Catholic church was built near Henry Street and was known as the Old Chapel. In 1855, it was replaced by the Roman Catholic Cathedral (Basilica).

The first Methodist church in St. John's, built in 1815, was destroyed by the February 1816 fire. The present Gower Street church was opened for worship in 1896.

Sketch of St. John's in 1857 by William Grey. The Anglican Cathedral of St. John the Baptist is shown to the left. (S. H. Cowell Ipswich, England. Outline of Newfoundland History, *L. E. F. English)*

The first Presbyterian church ("The Kirk") in St. John's was opened on Harvey Road in 1843 and rebuilt after the 1892 fire.

The first Congregational church was built in the spring of 1777. In 1895, the Congregational church on the corner of Queen's Road and Chapel Hill was opened. It replaced the church which had been destroyed in the fire of 1892. In 1938, the St. John's Congregational Church members voted to join with the Presbyterians, and this was approved.

The first Salvation Army temple in St. John's was opened in 1886.

The first Seventh-Day Adventist church was opened in St. John's in 1896.

The first Pentecostal church in St. John's was opened in 1911. The first Baptist church in St. John's was opened in 1957.

A literature depot for the distribution of Jehovah's Witnesses materials was established in St. John's in 1930.

St. John's first synagogue was opened in 1931.

St. John's in fete around 1905. (*Guide to Newfoundland*, 1905)

Education in St. John's

First Grammar School in St. John's

St. John's first grammar school was established in 1800. The teacher was the Reverend Lewis A. Anspach, who later wrote *A History of the Island of Newfoundland.*

In 1824, the Newfoundland School Society opened a school in St. John's.

In 1827, the Benevolent Irish Society set up a non-denominational school which later became denominational. As St. Patrick's Hall School, it operated until its closure in 1999.

This school was taken over by the Irish Christian Brothers in 1876. In 1889, they took over St. Bonaventure's College, and in 1890 opened a new boys' school, Holy Cross, at Riverhead. Mount Cashel Industrial School and Orphanage was opened in 1898.

First Convent Schools in St. John's

The first convent school in St. John's was opened by the Presentation Sisters in 1833. In 1842, the Sisters of Mercy arrived and another convent school was opened in St. John's. Later, the Mercy Sisters opened St. Bride's College, Littledale, a day and boarding school for girls.

Growth of Other Schools

Following the passage of the first Newfoundland Education Act, other schools were established on a denominational basis in St. John's. St. Bonaventure's College, Bishop Feild College, Bishop Spencer College, Methodist College, and Prince of Wales College were the forerunners of Brother Rice, Gonzaga, Holy Heart, Bishop's College, Prince of Wales Collegiate, and Booth Memorial. St. Bonaventure's has become a private Roman Catholic school, and Bishop Feild College is now a public elementary school.

First St. John's Library

The first St. John's Public Library was opened February 14, 1823. Afterwards, the Athenaeum was established. In 1936, the Gosling Memorial Library was opened. The Dr. Hunter Library in the Arts and Culture Centre was opened in the 1960s.

The Royal St. John's Regatta

The first mention of a Regatta occurs in the *Mercantile Journal* for September 24, 1818. However, 1826 has been generally accepted as the official starting date for the St. John's Regatta, held on Quidi Vidi Lake. It is the premier annual sporting event held in St. John's and thousands attend. Games of chance and a carnival spirit make it a great event for old and young alike.

B.I.S. Dramatic Troupe in 1906. (B.I.S. Centenary Book)

Government House Built

From 1729 to 1779, the Governors resided on board their warship in St. John's Harbour. In 1779, a house on York Street became the Governors' residence. Then the Governors resided at Fort Townshend from 1781 until 1831, when Government House was completed.

Colonial Building and Government House. (Outline of Newfoundland History, *L. E. F. English)*

Hospitals in St. John's

The first hospital in St. John's was built in 1725 by the British Navy for the treatment of sailors serving on the Newfoundland station. It was situated about a quarter mile east of the Long Bridge. It was replaced by a larger building in the same area in 1779. Sick Bay Number 6 at Fort Townshend was in operation for the soldiers from 1878-1883. In 1805, a new military hospital was opened near the site of the Colonial Building.

In 1813, a new General—it later became the Fever—Hospital was built in what is now Victoria Park. It was burned by order of the city council in 1888.

A new hospital was established in a house on Palk's Farm, on Waterford Bridge Road. In 1853, the cornerstone of the Waterford Hospital was laid.

In 1870, the military hospital on Forest Road became a General Hospital and continued to operate until the opening of the Health Sciences Complex in 1978.

In 1922, St. Clare's Hospital was opened. It was operated by the Sisters of Mercy. The Grace Hospital opened in 1923. It was operated by the Salvation Army.

In 1935, the Rotary Club established a camp for children on Thorburn Road. In 1954, the camp became a hospital, and its name was changed to the Sunshine Camp. In 1964, the patients were moved to what had been the American High School in Pleasantville. The building was now called the Children's Rehabilitation Centre.

In 1966, the Janeway Children's Hospital was opened in the former American Base Hospital at Pleasantville. A new Janeway Hospital building was opened in 2001 adjacent to the Health Sciences Complex.

Beothuk Women in St. John's

In all, five Beothuk women are known to have resided for a while in St. John's. The first woman's name is unknown. She was brought to St. John's in September of 1803 by William Cull, who was paid fifty pounds by the Governor for his "trouble and loss of time." She had been taken captive in Gander Bay the previous winter. The woman was allowed to visit the shops and take whatever caught her fancy. She lived at the Governor's residence in Fort Townshend for a while and was then sent back to her people. She never returned to her people. It was whispered she was murdered for the presents that she had been given. However, William Cull fiercely denied this allegation.

Mary March. (Cochrane & Parsons)

In 1819, another Beothuk woman, Demasduit, or Mary March as the Europeans called her, was brought to St. John's. Her husband had been killed trying to free his wife. She died while on her way back to her own people.

In 1823, three Beothuk women, a mother and her two daughters, were brought to St. John's by John Peyton. They were returned to the Bay of Exploits where the mother and the younger daughter died. The older daughter, Shawnadithit, lived with the Peytons for five years and then in 1827 came back to St.

*Shawnadithit (1801-1829). The last known surviving Beothuk. She was buried in the Church of England cemetery on the Southside of St. John's. (*Encyclopedia of Newfoundland and Labrador*)*

John's. She died in 1829 and was buried in an unmarked grave near the old St. Mary's Anglican Church on the Southside. The location of her gravesite is unknown. She was supposed to have been the last surviving member of the Beothuk tribe.

St. Andrew's Society Founded

On February 25, 1837, the St. Andrew's Society was instituted, and it is still flourishing in St. John's.

St. John's as the Island's Capital City

In 1804, Governor Erasmus Gower wrote that St. John's was "no longer a mere fishing station...but a port of extensive commerce." In 1832, with the opening of the first House of Assembly in rented rooms, St. John's truly became the capital of Newfoundland. There was a bit of trouble about unpaid rent when on February 3, 1834, Mrs. Mary Travers refused to release the furniture of the House of Assembly, which she had had attached, until her rent was paid. In 1850, the Colonial Building was opened and it became the seat of government. In 1855, Newfoundland obtained Responsible Government which continued to meet in the Colonial Building until the advent of Commission of Government in 1934. In 1949, the Colonial Building again became the seat of government, until the opening of Confederation Building in 1960.

Incorporation of St. John's

In 1833, notice of a bill to incorporate St. John's was given in the House of Assembly. However, petitions against incorporation were many, and the bill was dropped in 1834. It was not until 1888 that St. John's was incorporated and the first municipal elections held on August 30, 1888. From 1934 to 1949, the St. John's municipal council was the most influential elected governing body in Newfoundland and Labrador.

Interior of Kavanagh's Drug Store, St. John's in 1906. (B.I.S. Centenary Book)

Election Riots of 1861

From 1832 until 1861, the citizens of St. John's were deeply involved in partisan politics. On May 13, 1861, a mob gathered in downtown St. John's to protest the election of two Harbour

Main members of the House of Assembly. The crowd became violent, and Colonel Grant and the troops were called out. When his men were attacked, Colonel Grant ordered them to shoot, and several citizens were killed and a number of others wounded. On May 18, two hundred and fifty soldiers arrived in St. John's from Halifax to help keep the peace. This was the last political riot in St. John's, until the attack on the Colonial Building in 1932.

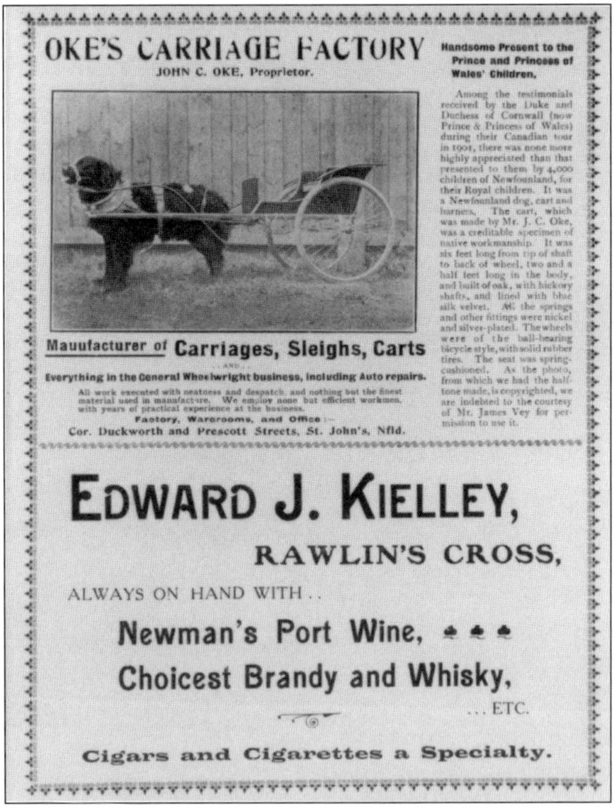

Advertisement for Oke's Carriage Factory (top) and Edward J. Kielley around 1906. (B.I.S. Centenary Book)

First Water from Windsor Lake

In the early nineteenth century, water was a scarce commodity in St. John's. Originally, there were no water tanks; springs, wells and little streams provided the people with water. Much of this water was impure and had an unpalatable taste. The main city wells were Bray's Well, Carroll's Well, Rennie's Mill River, Bell Chute, Garrison Hill Well, and Garrett's Well. At Beck's Cove, a Scotsman named McAusland constructed a reservoir that held forty puncheons of water. Around 1845, water was piped from George's Pond on Signal Hill. In 1859, a water company was established, and on June 16, 1862, the first water from Windsor Lake was turned on.

The Streets of Olde St. John's

Some of the old St. John's thoroughfares have long since changed their names or disappeared. One of these was Tarranhan's Town, which ran from St. Patrick's Hall to Prescott Street. It was destroyed by the fire of 1855. Tubrid's Town stood to the east of the Roman Catholic Cathredal, near Barnes Road. Dog's Town and Maggoty Cove were in the East End. Bell Chute, now Bell Street, and Pankins' Lane were in the centre of the city. Barking Kettle, Apple Tree Well, Pokeham Path, Lazybank, the Tickle, and Cribbie's were in the West End. Other old streets were Covel Lane, Delahunty's Lane, Dreelin's Well Road, Native's Lane, Kickham's Lane, Coady's Lane, Old Chapel Lane, Limeklin Hill (now Lime Street), Courting Lane (now Wickford Street), and Burstheart Hill (now Carter's Hill).

Water Street, St. John's around 1830, showing Kings Beach Auction Mart to the right. (Guide to Newfoundland, *1905, Prowse)*

A view of St. John's around 1920 showing St. Mary's Anglican Church on the Southside. (Courtesy of Mrs. Yvonne Humby)

Medical Society Formed in St. John's

Up until 1837, there were no regulations regarding the practice of medicine in St. John's. Anyone who wished could set up as a doctor. In 1867, the first St. John's Medical Society was formed to regulate the practice of medicine.

Quaint and Humorous Nineteenth Century Characters of St. John's

The Hermit

Over the years, St. John's has seen many strange characters. The Hermit was one of those people. A mysterious stranger, he lived in a tilt on Bay Bulls Road for six years and made his living by catching and selling trout. No one knew who the man was or where he came from. He dressed in workman's clothing, but he was clearly a scholar and a gentleman. On August 2, 1871, he took passage on a steamer for England. He arrived at the wharf dressed in the most fashionable clothes, with beaver hat, gold watch and chain, and rings. The man's identity has never been discovered.

Other Colourful St. John's Characters

There was also a whole bevy of other strange and wonderful characters, including Peggy the Poker, Kit the Hatter, Tom the Painter, Hallo the Hare, Paddy the Noggin, Foggy Dew, the Bishop's Hen, and the Racoon. There was also Micky Bottles, who always carried a brin bag to collect empty bottles. Nofty, who was forty and lost the pork, used to wheel his fish barrow through the streets and call out:

Salt herring fresh from Fortune Bay
Come this week by schooner May
If they're too late for your dinner
You can have 'em for your tea.

Johnny Burke, the Bard of Prescott Street, immortalized two other famous characters, Flipper Smith and Caroline Bowdin, in the "Kelligrews Soiree." Caroline always covered herself from head to toe with bright ribbons. She later married Flipper, who was described as a "gentleman of leisure."

St. John's Major Municipal Parks

The first municipal park to be established in St. John's was Victoria Park. In 1888, the old hospital which stood on the site was burned, and the land was then used as a park which became known as the West End Park. In 1889, the site was improved and renamed Victoria Park.

In 1891, a second park, Bannerman Park, was opened in the East End on September 1. It was next to Government House and named after Governor Bannerman.

Littledale students enjoy a boat ride in the duck pond in Bowring Park in the 1920s. (Courtesy of McCarthy family)

In 1911, Bowring Brothers donated a farm on the Waterford River to the city to be used as a park. This was to commemorate the centenary of the company. It was officially opened on July 15 by the Duke of Connaught. It has since been enlarged by the addition of the Sir Richard Squires property.

Earthquake Report

On July 23, 1890, the keeper of the blockhouse reported two earthquake shocks were felt at the blockhouse in St. John's.

Queen's Fort and Cabot Tower on Signal Hill, St. John's, early twentieth century. (Cochrane & Parsons)

First Transatlantic Signal

In 1901, Guglielmo Marconi received the first transatlantic wireless signal from England at Signal Hill in St. John's. He was unable to continue in St. John's because the Anglo-American Company held a monopoly on all electrical messages to and from Newfoundland, and they asked the courts for an injunction preventing Marconi proceeding further with his experiments in Newfoundland. The injunction was granted and Marconi left for Nova Scotia.

Memorial University College

This college on Parade Street was opened in 1925 and dedicated to the memory of the Newfoundland servicemen who died in World War I. It offered a three-year college program. In 1949, it became a degree-granting university. A new university campus on Elizabeth Avenue was opened in 1961.

The St. John's Riverhead historic railway station around the 1920s. The railway was shut down in Newfoundland and the last train ran on September 20, 1988. (PANL)

Street scene in St. John's around 1930. (*Peeps at Many Lands*, Fairford)

Establishment of Commission of Government

In 1934, Newfoundland gave up her Dominion status and reverted to a crown colony ruled by a commission of six appointed persons, three Englishmen and three Newfoundlanders. It was promised that when Newfoundland was financially stable, Dominion status with Responsible Government would be returned.

*Commission of Government in session around 1945. (*Story of Newfoundland, *Cochrane & Parsons)*

Britain did not honour the terms of the agreement and held a national convention to decide on what forms of government the Newfoundland people could vote for. In 1948, Newfoundlanders voted to join Canada by a small majority. Officially, Newfoundland became the tenth province of Canada at 11:59 P.M. on March 31, 1949. However, the anti-confederates always claimed that Newfoundland joined Canada on April 1, All Fools' Day.

Arrival of the Canadian Forces in St. John's

At the outbreak of World War II, St. John's was very vulnerable to an attack by German warships on the Grand Banks. In 1940, Canada established a naval base, two naval hospitals, and a barracks at Buckmaster's and Lester's fields. They also built the airport at Torbay to serve St. John's.

Arrival of the American Forces

In 1941, the United States built a large army base at Pleasantville on Quidi Vidi Lake and renamed it Fort Pepperrell. They also built a loading dock in the east end of the harbour.

There were around 10,000 American military personnel stationed in St. John's by 1944. It has been estimated that 40,000 Newfoundland girls married American servicemen during the life of the American bases in Newfoundland.

Confederation with Canada

From 1867 until 1948, Newfoundland rejected union with Canada, and although Newfoundlanders on a second ballot voted to join Canada in 1949 by a very small margin, the citizens of St. John's opposed this union and voted by a margin of more than two to one to restore Responsible Government. The entry into Confederation was a disaster for many smaller St. John's manufacturing industries, and many of them failed. The service industries, however, prospered. In 1967, to mark the hundredth anniversary of Confederation, a new Arts and Culture building was erected near the Memorial University complex.

Growth of the City

Today, the population of the city of St. John's numbers over 100,000 persons. In recent years, the adjoining communities of Airport Heights, Kilbride, the Goulds, Shea Heights and Wedgewood Park have become part of the city. In 1998, St. John's was confirmed in its possession of Southlands, a new development adjoining the neighbouring city of Mount Pearl.

St. John's from the Golf Links around 1934. (*Peeps at Many Lands*, Fairford)

Section II

Women in Eighteenth Century St. John's

A FEMALE SERVANT IN EIGHTEENTH CENTURY ST. JOHN'S.
(NEWFOUNDLAND LITERATURE READERS, BOOK V)

The Lieutenant's Mistress

In 1700, a St. John's lady became prominent in the social life of the town when she became the mistress of Major Thomas Lloyd, the commander at Fort William. In a letter to his religious superiors in England, the Reverend John Jackson, Church of England Chaplain at Fort William, condemned Major Lloyd for his sinful ways.

In his letter, Reverend Jackson pointed out that Major Lloyd had taken as his mistress a Mrs. Short, the wife of a St. John's inhabitant. With some heat, the reverend gentleman accused Mrs. Short of being a notorious thief and whore before becoming the major's mistress. He went on to say that to this rather disreputable lady Lloyd had given supreme authority and absolute power over the soldiers in the fort and the civilian population of St. John's. As well, he had built within the fort a special apartment for her, using the "Queen's timber."

In her new role as first lady of St. John's, Mrs Short was accused of taking advantage of her new social standing to get even with her former enemies. According to the parson, "Any one for whom she had the least dislike she caused to be whipped at her pleasure." As well, neither she nor Major Lloyd attended Sunday services, and, in fact, they made it difficult for other people to attend.

On Sunday mornings, Major Lloyd would take his fiddle and, accompanied by Mrs. Short, would go about the town and persuade as many persons as he could to join with him and Mrs. Short in dancing and other riotous behaviour. It was not just innocent dancing, however, that raised the parson's ire, and in graphic terms he painted a terrible picture of the moral laxity encouraged by the Major and his lady:

> He hath gone about the harbour on the Lord's Day with his fiddle on purpose to divert the people from coming to church. The rest of the day he revels away with his companions in dancing and rioting with their whores. Nay, which is worse than a beast he hath chosen such companions who have been so audaciously imprudent as to dance stark naked together to the shame of all modest parents.

The parson's complaint fell on deaf ears, and Thomas Lloyd remained commander of St. John's until 1704. In that year, he was recalled to England. He returned to St. John's in 1708 and again took command of the fort. The fate of Mrs. Short has not been recorded.

However, Sunday continued to be anything but a day of worship, for in 1711, Commander Crowe, Commodore of the English convoy, described a Sunday in St. John's:

> Before my arrival, the Lord's Day was nothing at all regarded, neither by the Inhabitants or common saylors who spent it generally in the Courses of Entertainment in Drinking, Swearing, and the Most Disorderly Actions, Living without any sense of Religion and prophaning the Day to that Degree that a stranger could never believe they had heard of Christianity, nor indeed of God, except by the Oaths, Curses and the Blasphemous Expressions, and horrid Imprecations. At my first meeting with Commanders of Ships and the Planters of St. John's, I represented this to them and proposed they should through voluntary contributions repair their church and do something for the maintenance of the minister sent by the Bishop of London who arrived at the same time with me. When the church was repaired and upon my publishing by Beat of Drum and affixing to the most public places the Laws established in England against Immorality & Prophaness & punishing those that were found guilty accordingly, their Swearing & riotious

behaviour was in a great measure left off & the church on that day generally frequented, had they a man among them empowered to put the laws into execution who would do it impartially & prefer the Public before his own private interests, Religion would soon be effectively established.

Three Violent Crimes Against Women in Eighteenth Century St. John's

The Flogging and Death of Christine

In 1704, Lieutenant John Moody took over command of the fort at St. John's from Major Lloyd. Moody was an Irish-born soldier of fortune who in the first year of his command ordered that a most cruel punishment be carried out on a young orphan girl named Christine, a servant of the Reverend John Jackson. The full horror of Moody's actions became known in 1706, when Commander John Winderdown of Her Majesty's ship *Faulkland*, Commodore of the Newfoundland convoy, and John Fry, Vice-Admiral of St. John's, held an inquiry into the events surrounding the death of Christine.

Lieutenant Moody had become very friendly with Margaret Jackson, the eldest daughter of the chaplain, and it was as a result of her complaint about Christine that she was punished.

It all began on a December morning, a few days before Christmas, when Margaret Jackson had words with Christine. According to later testimony, Christine answered her back and Margaret went to the house of Lieutenant Moody to complain that Christine had abused her. Moody immediately ordered Christine to appear before him. He asked her why she had abused her mistress, and Christine denied that she had done so. Moody then ordered that she be taken outside and fastened to a cannon.

After she had been secured to the gun, she was stripped bare from the neck to the waist and severely flogged by John Tyllyard, a drummer. Moody supervised the flogging, and after she had reccived a number of lashes he asked her again why she had abused her mistress. Christine, despite the pain and cold, answered she had not abused her mistress, that rather her mistress had abused her. Moody ordered the flogging to continue.

When the flogging was finished, Christine's back had been cut to ribbons, but the soldiers replaced her upper garments and fastened her to a wooden horse. Then, they lifted her hands and poured cold water down her sleeves with a funnel, which ran down her lacerated back while a soldier named Richard Oliver and the drummer, John Tyllyard, slapped her on her back with their hands in order that the water might better soak into her clothes. According to the testimony of John Wexford, a soldier who was present at the time, "It being a sharp frost was of so ill consequence, the water running clear under her clothes down her legs to the ground."

When the water treatment was completed to Moody's satisfaction, he ordered that Christine be thrown outside the walls of the fort to die of exposure. Having no place to go, Christine made her way to the house of Elizabeth Bunker, who did the washing at the Jackson house and had witnessed her punishment. Elizabeth took the poor girl in, and she and her husband Richard did their best to tend to her wounds.

The news that the Bunkers had given Christine a place of refuge was reported back to the fort, and Moody sent an officer named Colin Campbell to order the Bunkers to turn her out of doors.

If they didn't obey this order, he threatened to have their house pulled down. Richard Bunker replied that they paid rent for the house and he might do what he liked with it, but they had no intention of turning Christine out of doors. Campbell went away, and Moody took no further action.

According to the testimony of Mrs Bunker, Christine lived for fourteen days after the beating. Mrs. Susanna Marshall, a neighbour of Mrs. Bunker, testified that she had visited Christine after the whipping and water torture. The girl was in bed at Elizabeth Bunker's, and she told Mrs. Marshall that she believed the punishment she had received at the fort would be the cause of her death. Susanna Marshal also said she saw Christine's corpse after her death, and she was all black, from her neck down to her waist.

Altogether, eight witnesses testified before the inquiry, and all told the same story about the punishment. They also agreed that the whipping and water torture had brought about Christine's death. Elizabeth Bunker and Susanne Marshall also agreed that Christine had forgiven her tormentors before her death. Susanne said she prayed, "God forgive them that did it and were the occasion of it as I hope God will forgive me my sins." Elizabeth Bunker said she prayed during her illness that "God forgive those that caused me to be whipped, as I desire God to forgive me." A little while before her death, she also said that Christine told her, "I have no friend, but I hope I am going to the place appointed for me." Another time, she said, "I am sorry that you should be troubled about me, for after I am buried you will when the ships come in be examined about me."

Following the inquiry, the results were reported to the English authorities, but no action was taken against Moody. He remained in command of the fort at St. John's until he was replaced by Thomas Lloyd, who returned to St. John's in 1708. In 1713, Moody was promoted to the post of Lieutenant-Governor and commander of the fort at Placentia.

A female domestic servant in nineteenth century St. John's. (*Newfoundland Literature Readers*, Book V)

Elizabeth Melville and the Soldiers

Elizabeth Melville, a girl of seventeen, was servant to mistress Ann Moore, a resident of St. John's. On the eighth of July, 1751, Ann Moore, her friend Katherine Wheyland, and Elizabeth went in the woods to pick wild strawberries. While they were picking berries, they were approached by three soldiers. Later in court, Elizabeth described what followed:

> That on the 8th day of July last, she went with her mistress Ann Moore and her friend Katherine Wheyland to pick strawberries. While we was about the same, we saw 3 soldiers, one of which took hold of me by the arm and gave me a swirl around, and said "Damn you, you whore, lay down!" Upon which my mistress and Katherine Wheyland ran away. He then threw me down upon which I cryed out and desired him to let me go. "Damn you, you little Bitch, I won't 'till I please," he said. The other two soldiers came from the bushes, I then said to one of them, "I know your face again, he then said, "Damn you, I'll turn the other two back. The other soldier that came out of the bushes took hold of me by the arm, the first still having hold of the other arm, and I then desired the soldier that last took hold of me to let me go. He answered "I should," then the two talked Irish together, and the first that took hold of me said I should not go 'till he pleased. Then the first soldier had carnal knowledge of my body, the other holding me by the arms and head, and when he had done, the second soldier had carnal knowledge of my body, the first holding me down at the same time, during the whole time I cryed out, and they put their hands before my mouth. The other that went after my mistress and Katherine Wheyland I saw no more.

When they had finished raping the girl, they took her by the arm and led her down to the river below Mr. Keene's meadow and put the girl in the river. When she was in the river, one of the soldiers took a paper out of his pocket and told her that if she did not swear on the paper, which was part of the Bible, not to report them, they would drown her in the river. She said she could not read anyway, so the Bible made no difference and her word was good as her oath. They took her out of the river and attempted to have carnal knowledge of her body again.

Then, they said that if she would not agree to meet them again in another place, they would put her in fear of her life, and she, fearing them, agreed to do so in order to get away. Having succeeded, as they thought, in frightening the girl into submission, they now changed tactics and tried to be friendly. They offered to exchange their handkerchiefs for the ones she had on her head and around her neck. She told them she couldn't change, as hers belonged to her mistress, and one of them said, "Damn the old bitch. If we come athwart of her, we will kill her!"

The last thing they did was ask to exchange the ring she was wearing, but when she said no, they did not insist and let her go, confident that she would be afraid to inform on them.

As soon as she got home and told her mistress, Ann Moore, what had happened, her mistress sent for Elizabeth's mother. All three women went to the fort, and Elizabeth laid a complaint before Governor Bradstreet and described the men who had molested her.

Governor Bradstreet then called in several soldiers who fitted the description given by Elizabeth. She identified Michael Ryan and William Fielding as the two men who had molested her. A third suspect, Philip Coffee, was released after Elizabeth failed to identify him.

Governor Bradstreet urged Elizabeth to be careful in making her identification, as she did not know what it was "to swear away a man's life." Elizabeth showed great spirit and said that if he, Bradstreet, would not give her justice, she would take it upon herself to stick a knife in her tormentors. The Governor then ordered the two accused men to be confined in the black hole of the fort until their appearance in a civil court.

When the two men came to trial, a number of witnesses swore that Michael Ryan had been in their company that day. As well, a woman named Margaret Gilbert swore that Ryan had been in her house at the time the attack was made on Elizabeth. As a result, the jury returned a verdict of not guilty for Michael Ryan, and he was released.

During the trial, Ann Moore testified that she had at first faced the soldier, but he threatened to knock her brains out.

When she saw the other two soldiers coming, she ran away. However, she saw her servant held by one of the soldiers and heard her calling out, "Oh, my dear mistress!" Katherine Wheyland testified the soldiers approached them and asked, "Shall we pick berries for you, pretty girls?" When Mrs. Moore said they had berries enough, they seized on Elizabeth and she made her escape.

No one defended William Fielding, and he was found guilty of rape and sentenced to be hanged. However, the sentence was later commuted and he was sent out of the island.

Ann Coffin and her Servant Mildred Bevill

The death of Christine in 1704 shows clearly that the life of a female apprentice or servant could be one of pain and terror, sometimes ending in death. Another incident of the ill treatment of a servant girl that led to her death in 1752 shows that conditions had changed little since 1704.

Mistress Ann Coffin was the wife of John Coffin, a respectable planter who kept a small shop in St. John's. Mildred Bevill was an orphan girl who was apprenticed to Mistress Coffin. On April 13, 1752, Mildred Bevill died at the house of Edward Wheyland, where she had been removed for treatment of her dropsy and various wounds that her mistress, Ann Coffin, had inflicted on her.

On the day she died, the members of the grand jury viewed the many bruises on her body, and Ann Coffin was committed to stand trial at a court of Oyer and Terminer. She came up for trial early in 1753 and was charged with having caused the death of her servant, Mildred Bevill. She pleaded not guilty to the charge, and the trial proceeded.

The Crown called a number of witnesses who testified concerning the way Ann Coffin treated her servant.

The first witnesses were two ladies named Margaret Ridley and Ann Moore. They had been called upon to view the body of Mildred after her death. They also declared under oath that they had seen Ann Coffin beat the girl a number of times with a stick, a poker and a pair of tongs. On another occasion, Ann had thrown Mildred to the floor and kicked her.

Another witness, Daniel Cox, testified he had seen Ann Coffin knock her servant down on the floor and give her five or six strokes across her back with the fire tongs. While she had been engaged in beating her, she had abused her verbally, calling her a "pocky bitch" and a "nasty Indian bitch." She also said that it would be no harm to kill an "Indian bitch."

Samuel Freeman, another witness, testified that he had heard Mildred say sometime in the fall of 1751 three or four persons had carnal knowledge of her body. One person, a tall fisherman whom she did not know, had grabbed her and thrown her down on a pile of rocks and raped her so violently that she had not fully recovered from the assault.

Margaret Ridley, a local midwife, was called and testified that she had been asked by Mildred's married sister, Elizabeth, to go to Edward Wheyland's house to see her sister. There had been a rumour spread abroad that Mildred was with child and suffered from the "foul distemper." Mrs. Ridley examined Mildred and asked her if she was with child. Mildred denied that this was the case. Mrs. Ridley then asked her such questions as she thought necessary, but Mildred appeared to be innocent and did not understand her questions.

The midwife then laid her hand on Mildred's belly, which was much swollen, and asked if she had met with any hurt. Mildred replied that her mistress, Ann Coffin, beat her. The midwife asked when was the last time she had been beaten. Mildred replied that it was the time the chimney caught on fire and her mistress beat her with the fire tongs. After beating her with the tongs, her mistress ordered her to go to a room, where she was beaten when there was company in the house. Ann Coffin followed her and with a short piece of wood beat her until she fell to the floor. Then Ann Coffin kicked her and stamped on her back. She then made her get up and tied her to a chair and beat her again before leaving the room. She was kept in this room for several days and fed only bread and water.

Mrs. Ridley finished her evidence by saying that, as far as she could tell, Mildred was neither with child nor had the foul distemper. The only disease the girl suffered from was dropsy, which caused the swelling in her belly.

Another witness, another midwife named Margaret Mitchell, said she had been with Mrs. Ridley during her examination of Mildred. After the examination, Mildred had asked to see her master, John Coffin. Ann Moore sent for him, and when he came he asked, "How are you, Millie?" Mildred replied, "Very bad." She then said, "God forgive you, and I forgive you." She asked that her things might be given to her sister's children.

Thomas Munn was called and testified that in February of 1752, Ann Coffin had told him she had given Mildred "her dressing," and Mildred later came in with a black patch on her cheek. About six days later, he saw Mildred lashed to the back of a chair which was overturned on the floor. He released the girl and she told him her mistress had whipped her several times that day with a cat-o'-nine-tails. When he asked Ann Coffin why she treated a motherless, fatherless girl so barbarously, she replied that she believed she "would be hanged for her at last."

The surgeon who had tended Mildred at the Wheyland's house testified that on one visit to see Mildred, Ann Coffin accompanied him. As soon as she entered the room where Mildred was lying, she began to abuse her, saying, "You bitch! You Indian bitch, you whore! How come you to belie me that I do not give you victuals enough?" She then suddenly seized Mildred by the nose and twisted it violently three times. Then Sarah Wheyland said, "Why don't you say it to your mistress's face?" When Mildred made no answer, Ann Coffin called her a "stinking Indian bitch" and caught her by the nose again. At this point, the surgeon, John Hendricks, said her arm was broken and she could not work for Ann Coffin. All Ann Coffin said was, "I hope it don't take her life."

Another witness, Richard Doyle, was then called to testify. He said that about a month before the girl's death, he was at John Coffin's house and saw Mildred at breakfast. He saw Ann Coffin kick the girl and then take her into another room, where she beat her with a stick about the bigness of his finger. He heard Mildred crying and sobbing, but her mistress kept beating her and calling her "whore and strumpet." Mildred cried and cried until it seemed she was too weak to cry any longer.

When all the evidence was in, it was apparent that there could be little doubt that Ann Coffin, by her systematic cruelty, had brought about the death of her servant. She was found guilty and sentenced to leave the island of Newfoundland by the first outbound vessel that would take her.

A Happy Christmas To You All **drawn by Lucien Davis reflects the joy of these two women during Christmastime. (Courtesy of Mr. J. Martin, MUN Photo and the** ***London Illustrated News*****. Christmas Number, 1898)**

Section III

Crime and Punishment in Eighteenth Century St. John's

In the stocks. (Cochrane & Parsons)

The Quidi Vidi Murder of 1754

Eleanor Power was an Irish girl who came out to Newfoundland and was a domestic servant in the household of Mr. William Keen, a St. John's merchant and magistrate. Magistrate Keen ran a very strict household. After supper and prayers in the evening, the domestic staff was supposed to retire for the night. Eleanor found it difficult to obey Keen's rules. She crept out after prayers one night and came home to find the door locked. She had to knock to be admitted, and Keen whipped her for her disobedience. Eleanor soon found a way to go out at night and escape detection. She fixed the bolt on the back door so that it could be slid back by inserting a knife blade from the outside. In the evening, she would accompany the other servants to bed, but as soon as they had fallen asleep, Eleanor would creep down the stairs and go out, secure in the knowledge that she could get back in without anyone being the wiser.

She served out her time and then left Keen's service to marry Robert Power, a fisherman from Blackhead, a small settlement in Freshwater Bay near St. John's. After her marriage, she discovered that life with Robert was, if anything, worse than serving in Keen's household. He drank heavily, and Eleanor was forced to work on the fish flakes to support them. To augment her income, she also sold rum and spruce beer to the Irish soldiers who used to come to Blackhead to visit her.

One evening in the spring of 1754, Eleanor was talking about her life in old Keen's service and happened to mention that he kept a chest filled with gold pieces in his house. The money was for buying up prize ships brought in by the privateers. One of the soldiers present, an Irishman named Edmund McGuire, became very interested in Keen's gold. He said to Eleanor that, as she had worked in the house, she would know exactly where the chest was kept. Eleanor not only knew where the chest was; she also revealed her secret way of gaining entrance to Keen's house.

Almost immediately, they began to formulate their plan to rob the magistrate, and it was Eleanor who appeared to take control of the venture. She enlisted her husband, seven other Irish soldiers including McGuire, and two other residents of Blackhead, to carry out her plan. It was decided that the robbery would be carried out towards the end of August. On the evening appointed, Eleanor Power, her husband, Robert Power, five soldiers, Matthew Halleran, Edmund McGuire, Paul McDonald, Lawrence Lambly and Nicholas Tobin left Blackhead in a skiff for St. John's. The only person in the boat who wasn't part of the gang was Nicholas Tobin, and Eleanor now decided to ask him to join them in the robbery. She made Tobin swear on a prayer book to join with them, and he took the oath.

They landed at the King's wharf, and here they were joined by another soldier named Hawkins, who led the way to Mr. Keen's summer house. A little later, they were joined there by John Moody and John Munshall, who also lived in Blackhead. Once again, all the robbers kissed Eleanor's prayer book and swore to be true to each other.

They waited in the summer house until midnight, and then Halleran, McGuire, and Lambly went out to see if the coast was clear. They returned rather hurriedly to report that there were a number of men splitting fish in the stage near Keen's house. On hearing this news, Eleanor decided to abandon the robbery for that night and said they would return to their homes and wait for a more favourable opportunity.

Around the first of September, they decided to try again. This time, the people from Blackhead walked in overland and joined the soldiers in Keen's summer house. Once again they were disappointed, for just as they were ready to enter the house, a skiff carrying Keen's son William, Jr. came and tied up at the wharf. The robbers judged there would be too many in the house for them to overcome, so they again returned home.

On the morning of September 9, Nicholas Tobin went out to Blackhead, and Eleanor told him to go back and inform the others that they would try again that night. Tobin returned to the fort and alerted the soldiers involved, and at midnight they again met at Keen's summer house. The robbers were armed with two muskets, two bayonets, and Robert Power had the broken tip of a scythe blade.

This time there were no people about, so Eleanor decided to go ahead with the robbery.

Nicholas Tobin and Robert Power were appointed watchmen, and each of them was given a musket, with orders to shoot anyone who tried to examine them too closely. Tobin took up his position near Mr. Squarry's house, which was next to Magistrate Keen's. Robert Power was to stand guard at the corner of another neighbour's house. Denis Hawkins was put on guard to give warning if anyone came near.

Eleanor had dressed in men's clothes for this occasion, and now she and McGuire, Halleran, Lamby, and Munshall entered the house by sliding back the bolt from the outside. McDonald was placed as guard at the door.

Then Eleanor and the four soldiers entered the house. Eleanor led the way to the place where the gold was supposed to be, and they emerged from the house in a few moments carrying a heavy chest. Lambly and Halleran also helped themselves to a number of silver spoons.

They took the chest to the summer house and forced the lock. However, the chest did not contain gold, but rather Keen's choice French wines and brandy. The robbers were very disappointed but consoled themselves with a few stiff drinks. While they were drinking, Eleanor went off with Lambly. Denis Hawkins was for giving up and going home, but John Munshall took hold of him and said they should go back and find the gold. Ed McGuire agreed with Munshall and said he would shoot anyone who tried to go away. He also said he was sorry for not shooting Eleanor when she went away. McGuire said he would be revenged on Keen for having him whipped for being drunk and disorderly. Halleran joined in and said if they couldn't find the money they should force Keen to tell them where it was.

After a few more swigs of the brandy, the robbers, with the exception of Eleanor Power and Lawrence Lambly, went back into Keen's house. While the others stood guard below stairs, McGuire and Halleran went up to Keen's bedroom. He was sound asleep, and Halleran found a box under his bed. When Halleran was hauling the box from under the bed, Keen woke up and began to call for help. McGuire threw a quilt over his head, but Keen managed to free himself and sit up. He reached out and put out the candle that McGuire was holding and caught McGuire by the leg, calling out "help" and "murder." Halleran, who carried the tip of the scythe blade, struck Keen twice with it and bragged that it had done its business and Keen would not recover. To make sure the old man was dead, McGuire struck him with the butt of his musket. They then took the box of money and several silver buckles and joined the others downstairs. They then went off to share out the spoils.

Both McGuire and Halleran were sure they had killed Keen, but when his cleaning woman came in the next morning, she found him still alive. She raised the alarm, and two St. John's surgeons, Thomas Allan and John Burton, attended him. Although alive, Keen was mortally wounded and died about eight days later from his wounds. Before his death, he identified the robbers, and a detachment of soldiers were sent to Blackhead, where they found the money and Keen's silver.

All ten of the robbers were arrested and charged with felony and murder. At the trial, Nicholas Tobin turned King's evidence and gave a full account of the robbery and murder. Edmund McGuire testified that only he and Halleran had been in the room when Keen was murdered. Robert Power and Eleanor both testified, saying they had nothing to say in their defence, except that they were not guilty of murder. Several of the robbers testified that Robert Power had been in favour of killing Keen, but Power denied this charge.

When all the evidence was in, the jury brought in a verdict of guilty, and the prisoners all threw themselves on the mercy of the court. The judge then pronounced the following sentence:

> That you Edmund McGuire, Matthew Halleran, Robert Power, Eleanor Power, Lawrence Lambly, Paul McDonald, John Moody, John Munshall and Denis Hawkins be sent back to the place from whence you came and from thence to the placc of execution and there be hanged by the neck until you are dead, dead, dead, and may the Lord have mercy on your soul.
>
> And that Edmund McGuire and Matthew Halleran after being dead and taken down are to be hanged in chains in some public place when and where the Governor shall be pleased to appoint.

On October 10, 1754, Halleran and McGuire were hanged, and their bodies were then hung in chains on Gibbet Hill. The next day, Eleanor Power and her husband Robert were both hanged together on Keen's wharf. Their bodies were taken down and buried near the place of execution.

Eleanor Power was the first woman to be hanged in Newfoundland, and after 1949 she became the first woman to have been hanged in Canada. Following her execution, a story was spread abroad that her ghost was seen in Keen's house in Quidi Vidi.

A Scoff of Beef in 1750 and Its Consequences

Catherine Keef was in domestic service in the house of William and Margaret Gilmore of St. John's. In September, 1750, she became involved in a case of possession of beef which had been butchered illegally and testified against her master.

The story began on the night of August 17, 1750, when four soldiers, David Williams, Richard Sutcliff, Mick Hayes and George Gardner butchered a cow which was grazing on the barrens near the town. They then carried the quarters of the meat to William Gilmore's house. Gilmore took the meat and hid it on his property. However, the crime was discovered, and the four men and William Gilmore were arrested and charged with the crime. On August 19, 1750, Catherine Keef gave a statement to Mr. Michael Gill, a Justice of the Peace for St. John's. Her testimony was later read in court, and she swore it was true.

In her sworn statement, Catherine said that she had been going into the fort after the barber, when she heard Mick Sutcliff say to his friend Dave Williams, "I don't know what I will do." Dave Williams answered him, saying, "By God, if it is found out, we will be hanged." Then the two men moved off the bridge, and she heard nothing else. Catherine also testified that a knife found near the remains of the cow belonged to her master, William Gilmore, and had been missing for four days. She further testified that the four soldiers had been at Gilmore's house on the morning when the cow had been killed. She also revealed that Gilmore sold liquor to the soldiers who came to his house, and on that morning Dave Williams had drunk half a pint of rum.

Later in the evening, the four soldiers were again in Gilmore's house, and Dave Williams called Mrs. Gilmore, William's wife, out of the kitchen, and they went into the bedroom. When Mrs. Gilmore came out, she said she would wristband Dave Williams's shirt and wash and iron it, as he had requested. Williams said he would call for the shirt or have it picked up in a little while. The soldiers left, and Mrs. Gilmore told Catherine to clean the pot, as she expected some people for supper. Catherine told her mistress there was no need to clean the pot, as there was a fish chowder in it for supper. Mrs. Gilmore ignored her and said again she expected company for supper.

Shortly after this, two Scottish seamen came in from the ship *Diamond* and bought some shirts and gave Margaret Gilmore half a crown and one dollar. Then they gave Catherine a shilling to go and get some rum, and her mistress sent her to Kate Tybol's to fetch it. After fetching the rum, Catherine went out, because she told the magistrate she knew Richard Sutcliff would be there, and he had often offered indecent things to her and had told her he would be at Gilmore's that evening.

Later, she peeked in the window, and the four soldiers and two Scotsmen were at supper. After supper, the two Scotsmen came out, and one took her handkerchief and put his own in its place. Then they went into the Gilmore house again as the soldiers had left. A short time later, the two Scotsmen left and went to Kate Tybol's.

Sometime later in the night, the four soldiers came back and knocked at the window. They called out three times to Gilmore. Gilmore's wife protested and said nobody should come into the house, and that she would never stretch by her husband's side again, for he was harbouring thieves. Gilmore's answer was to call his wife "a bitch!" and strike her on her ribs. Then he got up and let the soldiers in. She went on to say they stayed until dawning, and she heard them cutting up something, which, by the sound, seemed to be victuals.

The next morning, James Forrester brought a knife and asked Mrs. Gilmore if it was hers. She said she owned a similar knife, but couldn't be sure, but carried it to her husband, who said it was his knife. Then Forrester told Gilmore that he would come to hurt if the knife was his, for it was the knife that had killed the cow on the barrens last night. Gilmore's brave reply was, "If it killed twenty cows, it would still be my knife."

Forrester went away, taking the knife with him, and Mrs. Gilmore began to cry, saying that her husband had brought shame and disgrace on her, all on account of liquor. At this, Gilmore got out of bed and took some fresh beef out of a pork cask and hid it in a pile of wood in the garden. When he had finished, he came to Catherine and said, "Kate, if this thing should be known, you can take an oath that you did not see me out of my bed for the night." Catherine replied that she would only swear that she saw him at supper, and once when he let the other persons in the house. Then he went and put some stones over parts of beef which were hidden in the well and ordered her to put the pork cask over the well, which she did.

Two of the soldiers involved, George Gardner and Mick Hayes, gave evidence for the Crown. They testified that it was Dave Williams who had actually killed the cow. They also said it was William Gilmore who had said they should kill a cow or a calf or a sheep. Mick Hayes said it was bad advice, but

Gilmore said no one would know who did it, for he would hide the meat in his house. The two witnesses then described how they brought the meat and Gilmore hid it. He mentioned that a lamb had also been killed the night before the cow had been killed and the meat taken to Gilmore's house.

Then Mick Hayes said that he had caught the lamb, and that George Gardner had killed it. They brought the meat to Gilmore's house and gave it to his wife, Margaret. She took the meat without asking any questions and told the four soldiers to come back for supper around eight o'clock. After supper, they made two cans of "flip," a mixture of spruce beer and rum heated with a hot poker, and drank it. Then they were for going and finding Catherine Keef, but Gilmore said they would do better to kill a cow and gave them his knife. Hayes went on to say he held the cow and George Gardner hit the cow between the horns with a hatchet and knocked her down. Then Dave Williams butchered the cow with the knife they had been given by Gilmore. He confirmed Catharine Keef's testimony about their coming to Gilmore's house with the meat.

When the testimony was finished, the judge asked the prisoners if they had anything to say. They all said that William Gilmore had given them the knife and hatchet to kill the cow, and that they were much in liquor when they killed the cow, and they asked for mercy.

The jury retired for three quarters of an hour, and then brought back a verdict of guilty against the four soldiers and William Gilmore. The judge then sentenced them all to death, but added that Dave Williams and Richard Sutcliff should be recommended to the Governor for mercy.

A Matter of Mutton in 1759

Another case concerning the illegal killing of a lamb and the disposing of its meat came before the courts on September 12, 1759. This time, it was two well-known ladies of St. John's, Margaret Power and Katherine Shea (alias Cumming), who were indicted by the grand jury of Newfoundland in the following charge:

> The jurors of our Sovereign Lord the King, upon oath present Margaret Power and Katherine Shea (alias Cumming) that they resided in the same house as William Kitchin (he had been charged with killing a lamb) that the said Margaret Power and Katherine Shea did know of the said lamb being killed and brought into the said house and that they were accessories of the same by endeavouring to conceal the above lamb, which being against the peace of our Lord the King, his Crown and his Dignity.

William Kitchin pleaded guilty and threw himself on the mercy of the court. The two ladies pleaded not guilty and said they would be tried "by God and by their country."

The only witness was one of the town's constables. He told the court how he had gone to the house owned by Mary Aldridge, where Kitchin, Power, and Shea lived. While there, he saw Kitchin take a part of the lamb from the bed where Katherine Shea was sleeping. The meat was wrapped up in pea stocks, but he could not say whether or not Katherine Shea was an accessory or not. There being no other evidence given, the jury retired and brought in a verdict of not guilty for the two accused women, and they were dismissed.

Two Notorious St. John's Ladies of Eighteenth Century

In the late eighteenth century, there were two enterprising ladies in St. John's who did washing and baked bread and offered other comforts for some of the ships' crews in the harbour. However, at least in one case, they fell foul of the law.

On September 5, 1780, Catharine Connel and Mary Power were hauled into court and charged with keeping a disorderly house and illegally selling liquor. They were accused of having gone on board a vessel named the *O'Sean*, which was berthed in the harbour the previous day, under the pretext of collecting money for baking bread and washing the clothes of the crew.

The court asserted that this was not the real purpose of their visit to the ship. Instead, they had secreted liquor about their persons, which they sold to the crew of the *O'Sean,* along with other favours. The two ladies, the court claimed, were known as "bad people," having previously kept disorderly houses and disobeyed the Governor's instructions concerning liquor to sailors.

They pleaded innocent to the charge but were found guilty and fined ten pounds each.

On Pain of Being Whipped Every Monday

*Eighteenth century justice at the whipping post. (*The Story of Newfoundland, *Cochrane & Parsons)*

At a court held in St. John's in 1777, Patrick Knowlan, a resident of St. John's, was charged with stealing a counterpane from Peter Prim, a respectable St. John's merchant. He was found guilty as charged, and his punishment was:

> To be whipped by the common whipper with a halter about your neck, that is to say you are to receive 20 lashes at the common whipping post, then to be led by the halter to the Publick Path just opposite Mr. Peter Prim's door and there receive 20 lashes as before, and then led as before to the Vice-Admiral's Beach and there receive 20 lashes as before; to forfeit all your goods and chattels; to pay the charges of the court and to depart this island by the first vessel bound for Ireland, never to return on pain of having the same punishment repeated every Monday morning; to be kept in prison til you go aboard.

Two Nineteenth Century Duels in St. John's

There are only two duels recorded in the history of St. John's. Both of them occurred in the nineteenth century. The first one, on the afternoon of March 30, 1826, was fought between two army officers then stationed in St. John's and ended in tragedy. The second was between two jealous Newfoundlanders and ended in a fistfight.

The Duel of March 30, 1826

On the afternoon of March 30, 1826, Ensign John Philpot and Captain Mark Rudkin, two English officers stationed in St. John's, met to settle a debt of honour. The location chosen for the affair was West's farm, about a mile outside the city near Rennie's River Bridge.

The affair had its beginning at a card game, in the home of Captain Matthew H. Willock on the night of March 29, 1826. Ensign Philpot was in a bad mood and made a great row over who had won a pot of two pounds, eight shillings, and six pence. Captain Willcock asked Philpot to leave and suggested he should apologize to Captain Rudkin. Philpot refused, and grabbing a jug of water, he threw it over Rudkin and kicked him. The other officers tried the next day to get Philpot to apologize, but he refused, and so Rudkin challenged him to a duel.

The seconds of the two duellists marked out the ground, then each man took a pistol, and one of the seconds was chosen to give the order to fire. When the order rang out, both men fired. Philpot was considered a good shot, but Rudkin was an expert marksman. In this first round of shooting, Philpot grazed Rudkin's coat collar, and Rudkin had fired into the air.

The seconds tried to end the matter, but Philpot demanded a second shot. This time, Rudkin's bullet found its mark, and Philpot fell, mortally wounded. He died a little while afterwards. As duelling was considered murder in Newfoundland, Rudkin went into hiding but gave himself up when his seconds were arrested.

At his trial, Chief Justice Tucker was out for blood, and when the jury brought in a verdict of "Guilty, but without malice," he sent them back, demanding that they drop "without malice clause." In twenty minutes, the jury returned a "Not guilty" verdict, and Rudkin was released. Tradition has it that Rudkin left Newfoundland and returned to England, where he made provisions to support Philpot's mother, as her son had been her sole support.

For many years after the fatal duel, the road running across the stream was avoided after nightfall. For at a point close to the wooden bridge, where Rudkin's horse shied three times on his way to the duel, the restless ghost of Ensign Philpot was said to flit about, with one single blood-red spot upon his breast, shaped like the ace of hearts. These ghostly sightings have persisted well into the twentieth century.

The Duel of September 25, 1873

The 1826 duel ended in tragedy. A duel fought in the Fort Townshend Hollow between two young men vying for the affections of a young lady had a more comical ending.

Dennis Dooley had come over from Heart's Content and began to pay attention to a beautiful young St. John's belle. Gus Healey, a native of St. John's, considered that the young lady in question was his girl. Relations between the two young men became so strained that at last they both felt that only a duel to the death could settle the matter.

The two men chose their seconds; they made all the arrangements, with Fort Townshend Hollow being chosen as the appointed meeting place. On the afternoon of September 25, the two men met at the hollow to settle the matter as gentlemen.

The seconds presented the pistols, and at the given command by one of the seconds, the duellists turned and fired. Nothing happened, for the seconds had removed the live cartridges from the pistols and replaced them with blanks. The only noteworthy event of this meeting was that Dooley fainted with fright after firing. As the matter of who should have the right to court the young belle was still unsettled, the two men met at John Casey's barn on Flower's Hill to settle the matter by fisticuffs. A song was later composed about the duel:

On Friday last at half past two,
two love stricken chaps,
Up in Fort Townshend Hollow,
met for satisfaction raps;
One of them Gus Healey was,
the other Dooley Din.
Came over here from Heart's Content,
Miss 'Blank' green heart to win.
John Sullivan the 'bobby' fop,
turned six policemen out,
Wheeled to thc pistolizing sound,
right round to left about;
With pistols lowered beneath their arms,
they hied to Casey's Farm
Where Dooley Din got well oiled off
behind John Casey's barn.

As a footnote to the story, the young belle who caused the fight repulsed both of their advances and married another man.

The courthouse in St. John's, whose cornerstone was laid by His Majesty King George V, then Duke of York, on October 24, 1901. The building opened on May 2, 1904. (Photo by Garry Cranford)

Section IV

Flaming History: Fires in St. John's

THE BRAVERY AND DEDICATION OF THE ST. JOHN'S FIREFIGHTERS IS QUITE EVIDENT AS THEY FIGHT A BLAZE IN THE FORMER GREAT EASTERN OIL BUILDING ON WATER STREET WEST, ACROSS FROM ADELAIDE STREET. (COURTESY OF MR. T. CLANCY)

The Fire of December 21, 1708

The first recorded mention of a fire destroying a number of houses in St. John's appears in a letter from William Keen, a St. John's merchant, to the English authorities, describing the capture of the town by the French in the early morning of December 21, 1708. According to Keen's letter, on the evening of December 21, 1708, a fire of unknown origin burned two streets of houses in St. John's before it was put out.

The Nineteenth Century Fires of St. John's

The Fires of 1816

On Monday, February 12, 1816, the town of St. John's was ravaged by a disastrous fire which broke out about eight o'clock in the night in the centre of the town, and, fanned by a southeast gale, soon spread in all directions. The narrow streets and huddled wooden buildings made it impossible to stop the blaze. It burned for about six hours, destroying everything along the Upper and Lower Paths. It levelled 130 dwelling houses and left about 1,500 persons homeless.

As many of the stores destroyed contained the provisions to feed the 10,000 citizens of St. John's, Governor Francis Pickmore immediately ordered the merchants of the town to furnish a statement showing what supplies had been destroyed and what were still available. An account of the disaster was also sent to Lord Dalhousie in Halifax, making known the danger of starvation in St. John's during the ensuing winter and asking for the immediate supply of bread and flour to tide the people over the winter.

The losses from the 1816 fire were said to be at upwards of 100,000 pounds sterling. The 1,500 homeless people had to seek shelter on board ships in the harbour or wherever they could find lodgings. Thanks to Governor Pickmore's exertions and the generosity of Halifax and Boston, starvation was averted, and in the spring the work of rebuilding was begun.

The Benevolent Irish Society of St. John's was also very active in helping provide relief for the fire sufferers. A few days after the fire of February 12, the members of the Society met and discussed how best to render assistance. At the meeting, they voted 150 pounds from the funds to the Society's Committee of Charity to meet immediate needs. Other funds were made available but held in reserve for emergencies. As well, 500 pounds were made available to provide loans to Society members who had lost their houses in the fire to help them rebuild their homes.

One of the results of the fire of 1816 was that in spring, when the usual flow of Irish immigrants began arriving, St. John's was unable to accommodate them because of the lack of housing. Many of them then went to the outport towns. It was around this time that a large number of Irish settled in Placentia, Conception Bay and Bonavista Bay.

The Fires of November, 1817

While Governor Pickmore and the residents of St. John's were trying to rebuild after the February 12 fire of 1816, a second fire ravaged the town. It broke out about 10:00 P.M. on November 7, 1817, in a small house contiguous to Water Street. The fire, fanned by brisk winds, soon spread to the adjoining buildings, and soon Water Street was burning. It was on this street that the great depot of stores and provisions were situated. Although the citizens of St. John's battled the fire, aided by the military, it burned for over six hours, and when it finally burned out, 142 dwelling houses were in ashes. Many of the wharves and storehouses along Water Street were also destroyed, including the courthouse and the prison. Damages were estimated at 500,000 pounds.

In order to secure the prisoners who were in jail at the time, Governor Pickmore had a part of the garrison set up as a prison, and the convicts were transferred there. He also encouraged the citizens of the town to mount night patrols to prevent looting and vandalism.

However, the main problem facing Governor Pickmore and the citizens of St. John's was how to provide food for the 10,000 homeless, with so many of thc winter stores having been destroyed by the fire. The Governor's first action was to place an embargo on the export of provisions from the town. His proclamation read:

> Whereas it having been represented to me, that in consequence of the extensive destruction caused by the late disastrous fire among the principal storehouses and depositories of provisions intended for the winter supply of the inhabitants of this town, an alarming scarcity may ensue, at a season of the year when it will be impossible to obtain adequate relief, I have thought fit to impose a temporary embargo upon the export of provision from the port of St. John's, until the extent of the evil can be ascertained, and such measures adopted as the exigencies of the case may require. I, the Governor, do therefore by virtue of the power and authority in me vested, issue this proclamation, forbidding any ships, vessels, or boats of any kind or description to depart from the said port of St. John's without first obtaining my special authority and license for so doing.
>
> Francis Pickmore.

Besides issuing this proclamation, Governor Pickmore asked the merchants who had suffered fire damage to furnish an account of what articles of food they had been able to save. The merchants who had escaped the flames were also asked to furnish an account of what articles and stores they had on hand. The Governor also sent a message to Lord Dalhousie in Halifax, telling of the fire and asking that he give orders for the immediate dispatch to St. John's of 100 tons of bread and 100 tons of flour.

The Fire of November 21, 1817

Scarcely had the Governor put his relief measures in place when another fire ravaged the town. It was discovered around 3:00 A.M. on the morning of November 21, 1817, when the persons keeping watch on board the men-of-war in the harbour saw flames burst from a merchant's premises on the lower side of Water Street, which had escaped the first conflagration.

The sailors raised an alarm, and the citizens of St. John's were roused to help fight the new danger. Though there was little wind, the fire spread quickly among the wooden buildings which contained much inflammable materials. All efforts to arrest the progress of the fire failed, and in a very short while the buildings on both sides of Water Street were consumed. The fire also spread northward, and fifty-six dwelling houses were destroyed. In a presentation to the Governor, the grand jury had this to say:

> By the conflagrations of the 7th and 21st of this month property to a very large amount has been destroyed, and upwards of 2,000 individuals, comprising nearly one-fourth of the inhabitants of this important town, are at this inclement season deprived of their habitations.
>
> Calamities so extensive would have been in our most prosperous times productive of severe distress, but on retrospecting to our situation for the last three years, during which period we have alternately suffered by fire, famine, by lawless outrage and numerous mercantile failures, which have greatly injured the commercial reputation of the town, the recent conflagration seemed only wanting to consummate our misfortunes. Several hundred men in the prime of life, without money, or the means of being employed, without adequate clothing or food, are at the hour of midnight wandering amidst the smoking ruins to seek warmth from the ashes and food from the refuse of the half-consumed fish. In dwelling houses the misery is little less. Many families, once in affluence, are now in absolute want. Their earnings during the

> summer months were not sufficient for their support in the only period when they can be employed in the fishery, and they are now at the commencement of winter without the means of existence. Within these two days, two men have been found perished of cold, and many hundreds must inevitably experience a similar fate if humanity does not promptly and effectually step forward to their relief.

This fire put the entire population of St. John's, which numbered about 10,000, in imminent danger of starvation, and appeals were made to Halifax, Boston, and London for help. They responded quickly, and on January 1, 1818, the American brig *Messenger*, under command of Captain Peterson, arrived in St. John's from Boston with a load of 174 barrels of flour, 125 barrels of meal, eleven tierces of rice, twenty-seven barrels and 963 bags of bread for the fire sufferers. The British Government also made provisions for help, and Halifax responded generously to Governor Pickmore's appeal.

Governor Pickmore died on February 24, 1818, and the task of overseeing the rebuilding of St. John's fell to his successor, Sir Charles Hamilton. He arrived in St. John's on July 20, 1818 and almost immediately had notices posted prohibiting the commencement of any building on the site of the old ruins until some plan had been adopted to protect the city from similar destruction in the future. However, it took two years before the British Parliament enacted rules for the widening of the streets and rebuilding of the houses destroyed in the fires of 1816 and 1817. Needless to say, some people could not wait to rebuild their houses, and some structures were erected on the old sites and were tolerated by the authorities because of the great need for shelter.

Under the new rules, it was laid down that the principal street, Water Street, should not be less than fifty feet wide, and the second main street, running parallel to the former, should not be less than forty feet wide. All cross streets intersecting at right angles to these two main streets were to have a width of not less than sixty feet. With these measures in place, St. John's was again rebuilt.

The Fires of 1833, 1839, 1840, and 1846

On July 7, 1833, the premises of Bowring & Sons were completely destroyed by fire which started on the premises of J. B. Thompson, three doors away. In all, fifty houses, valued at 80,000 pounds, were burned.

In 1839, the town of St. John's was again threatened by fire when a block of tenement houses on the north side of Water Street caught fire and burned. However, the fire was contained, and only fifteen of the houses were destroyed in the blaze. The following year, 1840, another fire destroyed the Exchange building and looked for a while as if it might do a lot of damage, but it was quickly put out.

On the ninth of June, 1846, the town was not so lucky when another fire broke out, and before it was over, three quarters of the town was reduced to ashes.

The fire started at 8:30 A.M. on Tuesday, June 9 in George Hamlin's cabinet shop on George Street, when a pot of glue overheated and caught fire. The flames spread quickly to Queen Street, and in a short while that street was a raging inferno. The firefighters made a stand to fight the fire at the corner of Queen Street and Water Street. They were unsuccessful, and the fire burned as far as Riverhead, where only a superhuman effort saved Newman's premises.

Then the wind changed to the west, and when the oil vats belonging to Bennett and Stewart caught fire, a goodly portion of the town was doomed. The Governor, Sir John Harvey, was on the scene and directed the firefighters. By his command, a Mr. Stabb's house on O'Dwyer's Corner was blown up to make a firebreak, but again this proved unsuccessful, and the fire continued on its path of destruction. The sixty-foot streets built after the 1817 fire were as nothing in the path of the devouring elements.

House after house and business premises after business premises fell victim. The convent of the Presentation Nuns on Long's Hill, the customs house, the courthouse, the theatre, the jail (where one prisoner was burned to death), and the two bank buildings were destroyed. By nightfall, only a forest of chimneys were left standing to mark what had been a bustling town. Out of sixty large mercantile houses in St. John's, only the Newman building at Riverhead survived the fire. One spectator at the scene described it in these words:

> We never saw a fire spread with such awful rapidity; the flames seemed actually to leap from roof to roof; and the noise of the burning mass could be compared to nothing that we ever heard, except the roaring of the cataract of Niagara. The crash of falling materials was heard above the deep sound of the advancing flames, as roof after roof fell in at short intervals.

As well, the oil stored in vats around the waterfront escaped into the harbour, and at one time it seemed as if the very harbour was burning. As a result, several ships and boats which had been loaded with goods for safety were burned.

To aid the homeless, the Roman Catholic chapel, the Orphan Asylum School, and the Native Hall, which survived the fire, were thrown open to give them food and shelter. However, many people had to stay outdoors, and the open ground in front of Government House was occupied by numerous family groups sitting beside the furniture and personal effects they had been able to save. Philip Toque says:

> It was a sad sight to see shivering mothers endeavouring to shelter their little babes and to hush them to sleep; while the cries of the older ones for food in many cases was answered by "wait 'til daylight and we shall try to get some for you."

It was estimated that the fire destroyed 2,000 houses, and a total of $4,000,000.00 property was destroyed.

Governor Harvey also took immediate steps to try and help the people. He ordered the House of Assembly to meet within six days and for a limited time placed an embargo on the exportation of provisions. He also sent a circular letter to the Governor General and Lieutenant-Governors of all the British North American Colonies and the British consuls at Boston and New York, describing the terrible disaster that had befallen the town.

He chartered two vessels and sent them to Halifax and New York to load provisions. The Governor's plea for help was answered quickly, and food and building supplies began to flow into the town.

At a public meeting in Halifax, 1,500 pounds sterling were immediately subscribed to the St. John's Fire Relief Fund. The money was used to buy provisions, and a ship was chartered to bring it on to St. John's. The Government of Nova Scotia also voted 1,000 pounds sterling, and this money was sent to St. John's. The governments of Prince Edward Island and Canada also sent large sums of money, as did the towns of Saint John and Fredericton. The Government of Quebec also sent a very large sum of money.

The Government of England responded generously, and 30,000 pounds sterling were sent to aid the fire sufferers. Queen Victoria sent a letter to the Archbishops of Canterbury and York, authorizing them to bring the plight of the St. John's fire sufferers to the attention of their clergy and congregations.

As a result of the generous support from inside and outside the colony, St. John's was again rebuilt. Once again, measures were put in place to prevent a reoccurrence of such a disaster. Among these safeguards were the requirements that all buildings in the business district be constructed of brick or stone, and that oil vats be confined to the south side of the harbour.

The Fire of 1855

There was a fire in Pokeham Path, now Hamilton Avenue, on July 30, 1855. Seven houses were burned, and only for the good work done by the firemen and the soldiers who were called out to assist the firemen, St. John's could have been levelled. Governor Darling was present at the fire, encouraging everyone to do their best.

The Fire of 1856

On July 15, 1856, St. John's was again threatened with destruction when a fire broke out on Garrison Hill. It started in the house of Mr. Kelland, a boot- and shoemaker, and quickly spread to the adjoining houses. After a hard battle, the fire brigade was able to contain the blaze. But before the fire was brought under control, twenty houses on Garrison Hill had been destroyed.

Flaherty's Fire, October 22, 1856

On October 22, 1856, another St. John's fire, known as "Flaherty's First Fire," destroyed one hundred tenement houses. The loss was estimated at $60,000.

Henry Street Fire of 1859

On December 7, 1859, there was another devastating fire in St, John's. It started in the area of Henry Street near the site of the old Roman Catholic chapel. It was touch and go for a while as the fire spread quickly, but through the combined efforts of the fire brigade and the citizens, it was contained to the Henry Street area. This fire destroyed twenty houses and left fifty families homeless.

The 1866 "Tickles" Fire at Riverhead

On July 17, 1866, there was a fire in the Riverhead, or West End, of St. John's. In this fire, twenty tenements burned, and a large number of families were left homeless.

The Southside Hill Fire of August 14, 1876

On August 14, 1876, and for several days after, the Southside Hill was on fire from Syme's Bridge to the Narrows. During the night, the fire attracted thousands of citizens by its wild grandeur. The smoke from the fire, the wind being from the west, filled the bay and in part brought about the wreck of the Spanish brigantine *Mayaquezzana*.

The Great Fire of 1892

For forty-six years after the fire of 1846, St. John's avoided another major conflagration. Then on Friday, July 8, 1892, another disaster struck. About 5:00 P.M., the Central Fire Hall answered a call to Mr. Tim O'Brien's stable at the junction of Freshwater and Penneywell Road. Here, a carelessly discarded match had ignited some hay, and the building went up in flames.

In the beginning, a couple of buckets of water could have put out the fire, but the water had been turned off that day to repair some pipes, and none was available. When the fire brigade arrived, they too were hampered by the lack of water, for the reservoir near the scene of the fire was found to be empty. The water here had been used in a practice drill a month earlier and had not been refilled. With no water, the fire brigade was helpless, and the flames from the burning barn soon spread to nearby houses.

The summer of 1892 had been hot and dry, and the smoke from nearby forest fires filled the town. Friday, July 8 was a very hot day, with the temperature at eighty-seven degrees Fahrenheit, and there was a strong breeze. This fanned the flames, and the fire spread rapidly. In fact, it was soon apparent that this fire was going to be a big one.

Realizing the danger, many people turned out to help the firemen, but with no water they were powerless to even slow down the progress of the fire. Soon it was apparent that much of the town was doomed. In the face of this danger, people gathered their household goods and stored them in places which they thought were safe, like the Anglican Cathedral, Gower Street Methodist Church, and St. Patrick's Hall.

However, unchecked, the fire raged on. One wall of flame descended Carter's Hill; another destroyed Harvey Street. Everything in its path was reduced to ruins or ashes, and the places considered safe were soon engulfed in flames. The fire swept over Duckworth and Gower Street, and Water Street fell victim. Three vessels in the harbour were burned: the steamer *Sharpshooter*; the brig *Dove*; and the coal hulk *Huntress*. Three other ships, the *Nellie*, *Ethel*, and *Prince Le Boo*, had a narrow escape when their sails caught fire, but they were saved.

In an account of the fire given in the St. John's *Evening Herald* of July 10, the area devastated by the fire was outlined:

The Rendell-Shea home, located at 82 Cochrane Street, survived the Great Fire of 1892. George Thomas Rendell, a prominent St. John's businessman from Devon, England, had it built in 1879. The home came into the possession of George Shea, Mayor of St. John's (1902-1906), who married Margaret Rendell, George Rendell's daughter. It was occupied by George Shea's son, Captain Ambrose Shea until 1972. Later it was purchased by Dr. Susan McCorquodale. It is presently owned by Bruce and Jane Blackwood, who have done substantial work to restore it to its original form. (Public Archives of Newfoundland and Labrador)

McBride's Hill after the fire of 1892. (St. John's City Archives)

> The boundaries of the burnt district may be particularly described; from Beck's Cove, up Beck's Hill, along Bates Street to New Gower, west along New Gower, up Carter's Hill to corner of Wickford Street, thence west to back of houses on east side of Good View Street, thence north to Cabot Street, thence up Carter's Hill to Le-Marchant Road and on to Freshwater Road, thence east along Freshwater Road and down Harvey Street to Roman Catholic Cathedral. Down Garrison Hill and along Military Road, thence along to Queen's Road, south to Fire Hall, thence south of Church of England Academy and east along Bond Street. Up Cochrane Street and along Military Road to King's Bridge Road, thence south down Ordnance Street to Temperance Hill, up Signal Hill (the fire destroying many detached houses in the neighbourhood thence west along Water Street, including all the waterside premises).

Two people are known to have died in the fire. They were Ellen Molloy and Mrs. Stevens. The fire raged all night, and people who had not lost their houses took as many friends and relatives as they could. Others who had no place to go settled themselves and their belongings in Bannerman Park and the Roman Catholic Cathedral grounds, waiting for dawn to break.

It was a scene of desolation that met their eyes when morning came. In the East End, only a small section of Hoylestown was left standing; the rest of the town was in ruins. A temporary telegraph station sent out the news of the disaster, and once again the response was excellent. The evening after the fire, a ship from Halifax, the HMS *Blake*, was on her way to St. John's with provisions and tents. Another ship, the *Ulunda*, left the same port a few hours later, loaded with relief supplies. The *Dominion of Canada* steamer arrived with $10,000 worth of supplies and a $20,000 cash contribution. At Montreal, the SS *Newfoundland* was

St. Patricks Hall school after the fire of 1892. (St. John's City Archives)

loaded with relief stores and sent to St. John's. The Government of Ontario sent $10,000. Cheered by this generous assistance, the people of St. John's took heart and immediately set about rebuilding their town.

In a few short years, a new St. John's had grown like the phoenix from the ashes of the old.

The Knights of Columbus Hostel Fire, 1942

On December 12, 1942, St. John's experienced a fire which, although confined to one building, resulted in a horrific loss of life. The Knights of Columbus Hostel on Harvey Road was destroyed by fire of suspicious origin.

The Knights of Columbus Hostel before the fire in December of 1942. (St. John's City Archives)

Each Saturday night, the hostel sponsored a dance for servicemen, which was broadcast over the radio station VOCM. The fire broke out about 11:00 P.M., and as VOCM was broadcasting the barn dance, the first alarm came over the air.

In the middle of a song there were cries of "Fire! Fire!" and then voices calling out over the crackle of the flames before everything went dead.

The ruins of the Knights of Columbus Hostel after the great fire in December of 1942. (St. John's City Archives)

The cause of the fire was suspected sabotage, but this was never proved. In the rush to get out, many people were crushed, and smoke inhalation killed a great many. When the fire was finally put out, ninety-nine bodies were found in the ruins of the hostel.

The Hull House Fire of 1948

The Hull House was a private nursing home at the corner of Springdale and New Gower streets. On the morning of February 10, 1948, a fire broke out, and as many of the residents were old and some bedridden, they did not get out of the burning building. When the fire was brought under control, it was found that thirty-three persons had perished in the blaze. One of the victims was 91-year-old Captain Lane, who had been skipper on the SS *Eric* when she was sunk by a German submarine on August 24, 1918, near St. Pierre.

On February 10, 1948 spectators view the ruins of a fire in the Hull Home, which was a private nursing home on the corner of Springdale and New Gower streets. Thirty-three (33) persons died in this tragic fire. (Courtesy of Mr. T. Clancy)

The Chafe Nursing Home Fire, 1976

The Chafe Nursing Home was situated in the Goulds, and like the Hull Nursing Home had a number of elderly guests, some of whom were confined to their beds. On December 26, 1976, a fire broke out, and in a matter of minutes, the wooden building was engulfed in flames. The staff did what they could to save as many lives as possible, but despite their heroic efforts, twenty-one senior citizens died in the blaze.

The Harvey Road Fire, 1992

On the evening of December 21, 1992, St. John's had its biggest fire since the Great Fire of 1892. The blaze broke out on Harvey Road, on a bitterly cold night, with a strong wind blowing. Only for the heroic work of the St. John's firemen who managed to contain the blaze, a large part of the city might have again been reduced to ashes. As it was, 100 people were left homeless, and more than a dozen business premises were destroyed on Harvey Road and Long's Hill.

The CLB Armoury as seen in the early 1950s. (Courtesy of Mr. T. Clancy)

The fire started in the wooden, eighty-two-year-old Church Lads' Brigade Armoury and quickly spread to the adjoining buildings. Among the business premises destroyed in the blaze were the CLB Armoury, the Provincial Social Service Building (built on the site of the K of C Hostel destroyed by fire in 1942), a Dominion store, Capitol Taxi Stand, Big R Restaurant, Johnny's Restaurant, Bert's House of Styling, Rock & Leather, Ziggy Peelgood's, Roma Pizzeria, Acropolis Restaurant.

Fire extinguished at building on the corner of Prescott and Duckworth streets around the 1940s. (Courtesy of Mr. T. Clancy)

Section V

Shipwrecks
In and Around St. John's Harbour

THE SEALING FLEET LED BY THE ARCTIC BREAKING THROUGH THE ICE OF ST. JOHN'S HARBOUR. MANY SEALING SHIPS WHICH WENT TO THE FRONT DID NOT RETURN. (SKETCH DRAWN BY SCHELL AND HOGAN FROM A SKETCH BY J. W. HAYWARD FOR HARPERS WEEKLY, APRIL 5, 1884)

Sailing Direction for Entering St. John's Harbour in 1843

Since the first of September, 1836, a lighthouse on Cape Spear has exhibited a powerful revolving light at 275 feet above the level of the sea, which in clear weather may be seen at eight or nine leagues off, and in ordinary weather at five or six. The light shows a brilliant flash at regular intervals of one minute.

Upon Fort Amherst, on the South Head at the entrance to St. John's Harbour, there is shown a brilliant fixed light, which may also from its elevation be seen at a considerable distance.

The Following Directions for St. John's Have Been Given by Mr. Owen

The entrance of St. John's Harbour is readily known by the blockhouse on Signal Hill on the North Head and Amherst Fort on the South Head. There is a sunken rock called the Vestal, 50 fathoms without South Head, with only 25 feet of water on it. This rock is about 10 fathoms long and seven broad. The marks for it are: Fort William, which stands within the harbour on the North Side open of the South Head, bearing N 39 degrees W; and the outer Wash-Bull Rock open with Cuckold's Cove Head, bearing 47 degrees E; the Wash-Ball Rocks join with the North Head; they are all above water and steep-to, therefore not dangerous. The course in the Narrows is NW by W, distance 370 fathoms to

> Chain-Rock on the North, and the Pan-Cake on the South side. Both these rocks are above water, and steep-to. Sixty-five fathoms within the Pan-Cake Rock, on the South shore lies the Little Pan-Cake, a rocky shoal, dry at low water; and 80 fathoms within the latter lies a sunken rock called Prosser's Rock, running off 30 fathoms from a rock above water, in form of a saddle, with 18 feet of water in the hollow, and only 5 feet on the outside. It is steep-to with 5 fathoms close to it. After you have passed Prosser's Rock, you may stand to either shore, as they are clear and steep-to. You may anchor in what water you please, from 8 to 4 fathoms of muddy bottom.

The tide of St. John's sometimes rises seven or eight feet; it is not regular, but greatly influenced by wind.

A Narrow Escape:
The Grounding of the Delight
August 3, 1583

The earliest account of the grounding of a ship in the Narrows is that of the *Delight*, commanded by Sir Humphrey Gilbert. The accident was described by Edward Hayes:

> Thus, after we met with the *Swallow,* we held on our course southward, until we came against the harbour called St. John, (original spelling) about five leagues from the former Cape of St. Francis, where before the entrance into the harbour, we found also the frigate or *Squirrel* lying at anchor; whom the English merchants, that were and always be Admirals by turns interchangeably over the fleets of fishermen within the same harbour, would not permit to enter the harbour. Glad of so happy a meeting, both of the *Swallow* and the frigate in one day, being Saturday, the third of August, we made ready our fights, and prepared to enter the harbour, any resistance to the contrary notwithstanding, there being within of all nations to the number of 36 sails. But first the General dispatched a boat to give them knowledge of his coming for no ill intent, having commission from Her Majesty for his voyage he had in hand; and immediately we followed with a slack gale, and in the very entrance, which is but narrow, not above two butts' length, the Admiral (*Delight*) fell

upon a rock on the larboard side by great oversight, in that the weather was fair, the rock much above water fast by the shore, which neither went any sea-gate (current). But we found such readiness in the English merchants to help us in that danger, that without delay there were brought a number of boats, which towed off the ship, and cleared her of danger.

St. John's drydock. (St. John's City Archives)

An Early Shipwreck in St. John's Harbour: The Loss of the Vulture August 1812

In August of 1812, the schooner *Vulture*, belonging to a Guernsey firm, went ashore while trying to enter the Narrows. A report by Captain Collins to the owners in the Channel Islands said the wreck was caused by the "imprudence of the pilot, who was attempting to beat through the Narrows." On one tack, the schooner went over too far on the Southside and lodged on a rock.

The crew escaped unharmed, and with the help of the other Guernsey ships' crews and 120 sailors from HMS *Antelope* the cargo was saved, and as the *Vulture* was a wreck, they also saved the masts and rigging. The hull was left on the rock where she had struck.

Later in the fall, when the flagship of the Newfoundland naval squadron returned to St. John's, the first lieutenant of the ship, with the help of eighty sailors from the warship, salvaged the hull and towed it into port. The hull was repaired and refitted with masts and rigging and then sold to a new owner.

James Cantwell and a Rescue at Cape Spear November 17, 1861

The lighthouse at Cape Spear, the most easterly point of land in North America, was built in 1834 and went into operation on September 1, 1836. In 1846, James Cantwell, who was at that time harbour pilot in St. John's, was appointed lightkeeper at Cape Spear. Tradition has it that Mr. Cantwell was recommended for this position by Prince Henry of the Netherlands, who owed his life to the courage and seamanship of this man.

Prince Henry was on a goodwill visit to North America in the 69-gun Dutch frigate *Rhine*. St. John's was a port of call on the tour, and the prince was expected to arrive in St. John's during the first week of August. However, when the *Rhine* had not arrived by August 6, some concerns were expressed for the safety of the visiting prince. For nearly a week, the weather had been foggy, with a very heavy sea running, and it was feared the Dutch warship might come to grief trying to enter the Narrows.

On the evening of August 6, James Cantwell went out to see if he could find the *Rhine* and guide her into port. At great personal risk, he searched the area around Cape Spear and came upon the *Rhine*, sailing very close to the rocks of the cape. Cantwell arrived just in time and piloted the prince into St. John's Harbour.

On their safe arrival, Prince Henry asked James Cantwell if there was any way he could repay him for his service. Cantwell asked that the prince recommend him for the position of lightkeeper at Cape Spear when it became vacant. Prince Henry agreed to ask the Governor, and in 1846, James Cantwell was appointed lightkeeper at Cape Spear. There has been a descendant of James Cantwell as lightkeeper at Cape Spear ever since.

In 1861, James Cantwell and his sons were responsible for rescuing part of the crew of the schooner *Salmah* when she came to grief on the rocks at Cape Spear on the morning of November 17, 1861.

Late in the evening of November 16, Cantwell noticed two vessels, the *Harriet*, owned by Bowring Brothers of St. John's, and the *Salmah*, which was laden with a cargo of provisions from the United States. Both vessels were lying at anchor, waiting for the seas to go down before they could risk entering the harbour. James Cantwell knew that although the two ships were now riding at anchor, before morning they could be on the rocks if the wind changed and blew up a gale. Accordingly, Cantwell and his sons decided to keep watch during the night in case something happened. He also prepared several stout ropes to be used to rescue people who might attempt to make it to shore.

In the meantime, the captain of the *Harriet*, who had also read the weather signs, sent a boat into St. John's and got a tug to come out and tow his ship to safety in the harbour. The captain of the *Salmah* decided to wait until daylight and then try to enter the port. Towards daylight, the storm which Cantwell and the captain of the *Harriet* had expected arrived. The wind freshened from the northeast, and the *Salmah* dragged her anchors and was slowly but surely driven in towards land.

When dawn broke, the *Salmah's* captain and crew could see the perilous position they were in as they neared the rocks of Cape Spear. Huge waves crashed with an incredible violence on the rocky shore. However, with the vessel dragging her anchors and the wind driving the vessel in, there was nothing they could do but hope and pray the anchors might catch before she struck. If she struck, then the men were sure it would spell certain death to try and scramble through the surging surf to the safety of the rocks above. It was at this crucial point that James Cantwell and his sons came to their rescue.

All through the night, the Cantwells had kept a lookout, and when they saw the *Salmah* begin to drift in on the shore, they made ready to try and save the lives of her crew. When daylight broke, they took the ropes they had prepared and

Early sealing ships prepare to leave St. John's for the front. (PANL)

went out on the rocks to see what they could do when the ship struck. They had to be careful, for the waves at Cape Spear often sweep high up the sloping rocks, which makes it dangerous to get close enough to help anyone struggling in the surf.

As the Cantwell men waited, poised to go into action, the deadly drama of the sea unfolded before their eyes. The *Salmah*, twisting and turning in the grip of the waves and totally at their mercy, was pushed relentlessly in on shore. Just after daylight she struck, and a few minutes later the force of the driving waves and pounding surf tore her to pieces. As she split open, her cargo of provisions, barrels of beef and pork, puncheons of molasses, and sacks of corn and flour were flung into the surging maelstrom. This added another element of danger for those trying to escape the doomed ship through the breakers, for the shoreline was filled with bobbing barrels, broken spars, and wreckage of every description, which the huge waves swept in and pounded against the rocks. The only gleam of hope for the men on the *Salmah* was the sight of James Cantwell and his sons, standing as far down the cliffs as they dared, fearlessly waiting to come to their aid.

As soon as the ship struck, the Cantwells, with no apparent thought of danger to themselves, rushed even farther down the treacherous sloping rocks and with the skill born of long practice were able to throw a rope to the men on the *Salmah*. It was caught and fastened, and a lifeline was now in place. But even with the rope to give them support, it was no easy task for the men to get through the boiling surf without being dashed to death against the rocks or crushed by the swirling wreckage. There was only one way to safety, and the men took it. They held tight to the lifeline and jumped into the pounding surf. At once, the Cantwell men began the task of pulling them to safety. Battered but grateful, one after another, the crew made the dangerous journey.

However, for three of the *Salmah's* crew, it was not to be; just as they reached the shore, they were engulfed by the churning wreckage which swept over the rocks where they had landed, and it crushed them instantly. The captain and the rest of the crew made it and thanked God for the courage and bravery of the Cantwell men who had saved their lives at great risk to their own. They later acknowledged that, but for James Cantwell and his sons, there would have been no survivors from the wreck of the *Salmah*.

St. John's Harbour blocked with ice, circa 1880-1890. (St. John's City Archives)

As each battered seaman was pulled to safety they were helped up to the lighthouse, where Mrs. Cantwell gave them hot drinks and food and put them in warm beds to ward off the ill effects of their harrowing experience.

Later, when word of the shipwreck reached St. John's, the newspapers of the day carried the story of the Cantwells's heroic rescue of the crew of the *Salmah*. The *Newfoundlander*, one of the major St. John's newspapers of the day, remembered the time when James Cantwell had rescued Prince Henry of the Netherlands, saying it was not the first time James Cantwell had acted bravely in saving human life.

There were no rewards for the Cantwells, nothing but the praise of the public and the knowledge that they had saved some of their fellow men from a watery grave.

A Terrible Tragedy in the Narrows: The Loss of the Maggie November 7, 1896

On November 5, 1896, the fifty-seven-ton schooner *Maggie*, skippered by Captain Blundon, left Brooklyn, Goose Bay, and Bonavista Bay for St. John's. The schooner carried 1,000 quintals of fish, 800 of which belonged to Captain Blundon. Besides her crew of eight, the ship also carried fifteen persons who had taken passage to the city.

At about 6:45 P.M. on Saturday, November 7, Captain Blundon had passed the Narrows in the offing and was sailing in from the eastward, with flowing sheets aboard and a moderate southerly breeze. Both lights on the schooner were burning at the time. James Power was at the wheel of the *Maggie*, and the vessel was being kept a little down to make the South Battery at the entrance of the Narrows. Some of the men were gathered aft, paying out the main sheet.

In the meantime, the SS *Tiber*, under the command of Captain DeLisle, was going out of the harbour on a voyage to Montreal. When the steamer reached the Chain Rock in St. John's Harbour, her lights became visible to the men on the *Maggie*. Immediately, the word was passed around that a steamer was coming out, and care should be taken to look out for her.

The *Tiber* kept on her course out of the Narrows, and the *Maggie* was kept upwind. The two vessels came closer and closer, and the people on the *Maggie* yelled for the steamer to keep clear. It was too late: the *Tiber* struck the *Maggie* on the starboard side, just aft of the mainmast, and cut through her, taking the stern right off the schooner.

There was total panic on the *Maggie* as five women and eighteen men struggled for their lives. Most, if not all, of the women as well as a few men were in the cabin at the time of the collision and were probably crushed to death on impact. The shock of the collision took the two spars out of the schooner, and she immediately filled with water and sank. Those who had survived the shock of impact were now struggling in the icy waters, fighting for their lives.

Some went under but struggled to the surface again and fought to stay afloat until rescue came. Others sank to rise no more. Two men, D. Diamond and Stephen Blundon, made their escape from the sinking schooner by getting on board the *Tiber*. Diamond made it up on the leash of the foresail, and Blundon ran up the rigging, caught a rope hanging over the *Tiber's* side and swung out on it, trying to raise himself up. Another man, Thomas Abbott, swung out on the same line, keeping Blundon down by reason of his weight. Diamond reached over the side of the steamer and caught Blundon by the back of his collar and drew him up to safety. Abbott lost his hold on the rope and fell back in the sea and was drowned.

Sailing ships stuck in the ice in St. John's Harbour, circa 1892. (St. John's City Archives)

In the meantime, some of the crew and passengers were trying to launch the schooner's punt, and they had almost succeeded when the foremast came crashing down and the foreboom fell across the punt, smashing it to pieces. Two other men, Power and Lethbridge, held each other's hands over a bundle of hay. As they struggled in the water, the hay turned over and Power let go. He was drowned and Lethbridge was saved.

As the spars and sails went over the side, a number of people struggling in the water were forced under and drowned. Captain Blundon, who was trying to keep his wife's head above water, witnessed her being dragged under by the foresail and could do nothing to help her.

After some confusion on the *Tiber*, a boat was launched and under the command of the mate set about trying to rescue those in the water. The boat was run in among the wreckage, and a number of persons were rescued. Three or four other survivors were picked up by a boat from a Brigus schooner. The survivors were brought in and placed in the East End Police Station. The boat from the *Tiber* then went back to the steamer, which was waiting out in the bay, and she continued on her voyage.

The persons rescued were: Captain William Blundon; Isaac Blundon; Levi Blundon; Stephen Blundon; David Diamond; James Lethbridge; Thomas Holloway; Julius Lane and his wife Clara, both Esquimaux. They were given hot drinks and wrapped in warm blankets and kept warm. A doctor came and ordered one man, Levi Blundon, to the General Hospital. He was taken there in the police station ambulance. When the others had been given new dry clothing from Mr. E. M. Jackman, they were taken to the Sailor's Home around 10:00 P.M.

The persons who lost their lives in the collision were listed as: Thomas Abbott, 20, married with no children; William Ash, 50, married with nine children; Annie Blundon, wife of Captain Blundon and mother of a large family; George Blundon, 23, single; Joseph Diamond, 35, married with two children; William Diamond, 73, married with five children; Sarah Gullage, 50, married with three children; Herbert Holloway, 18, single; Isabelle Holloway, 20, single; Christopher Lethbridge, 24, married with two children; Moses Lethbridge, 33, married with five children; James Power, 28, and his wife Rhoda Power, 20, no children.

Later, two boxes from the wrecked schooner were turned in to the police. The boxes had been picked up near the Chain Rock but showed signs of having been tampered with. David Diamond identified the boxes as belonging to his father, who had drowned, and himself. He said there had been two purses in the boxes, each of which contained money, a watch and chain, and a cash box containing money.

These valuables were now missing, and the police went to the house of one of the men who had given the box over to the police. After some hard questioning, they found the cash box under a flake and returned it to its owner, as well as some of the watches.

On November 7, the St. John's *Evening Telegram* took issue with its rival newspaper, the St. John's *Daily News*, over the *Daily News's* report that Mr. Morrison and Mr. Morine, two Tory politicians, had been among the first to reach the East End Police Station and ordered the clothes from E. M. Jackman for the survivors. The *Telegram* said that it was Inspector D. I. Grimes who had looked after the needs of the survivors, and that the Prime Minister, Sir William Whiteway, had been on the scene immediately and commended Inspector Grimes for taking such good care of the survivors.

The wreck of the *Maggie* in the Narrows was one of the worst marine disasters to occur in the entrance to St. John's Harbour. The staggering death toll of thirteen persons, four of them women, cast a pall of sorrow over the entire city.

A Cuckhold's Cove Wreck: The Loss of the Barquentine Stella January 17, 1904

The *Stella* was a wooden barquentine, 234 tons gross, 221 tons net; she was 121 feet, seven inches long, twenty-five feet, eight inches wide, and thirteen feet deep. She was built in 1872 and in 1903 was being used by Baird Gordon Company in the foreign trade.

Around six o'clock on the evening of January 17, 1904, Hans Jensen, a sailor on the *Stella*, reported to the Baird Gordon's watchman that the *Stella*, under the command of Captain Jones, had gone ashore at Cuckhold's Cove near Quidi Vidi. He had been sent in to St. John's to ask that a tug be sent to her assistance.

The watchman immediately contacted Mr. H. Baird, and the tug *John Green* was sent with a number of employees of Baird Gordon to help the crew of the stranded ship. The tug returned around 9:00 P.M. and reported that they found no sign of the vessel, and the heavy seas running in the area prevented them from entering very far into Cuckhold's Cove to make a search for any survivors.

On the return of the *John Green* from Cuckhold's Cove, a rumour spread about St. John's that the *Stella* had been lost with eight of her crew missing. Immediately, the relatives of the missing crew members made their way to Baird Gordon's wharf to ask for information. However, soon after the tug's return, another seaman from the *Stella* named Murphy reached town to say that the barquentine was gone, but that the captain and all the crew members of the *Stella* had made it safely to shore. On hearing this news, a number of men set out by land for Cuckhold's Cove to render assistance to the shipwrecked crew. A detachment of policemen were also dispatched to safeguard any salvage from the wreck.

The mate of the *Stella*, Mr. Martin, later told the story of her last voyage.

They had carried a load of fish to Pernambuco and on December 22, 1903 had left that South American port for St. John's. They had a good run up the North American seaboard and about 3:15 on the evening of January 17, 1904 could see Cape Spear quite plainly. They then decided to run for the Narrows. The wind was about southeast, quite strong, and accompanied by snow squalls. They shaped their course for the Narrows, and the squalls became less thick. But then the wind suddenly increased, and a heavy snow squall obscured their visibility. However, they decided that they were right on course for the Narrows and kept their way. Then around 4:00 P.M., without warning, the cliffs of Cuckhold's Cove Head suddenly loomed out of the snow directly ahead of them, and they were only a few feet from the rocks.

Immediately, they tried to bring the vessel around, but with so little seaway this was an impossible task, and she went ashore, striking the cliffs which tore away all her headgear and cracked the bowsprit. The ship finally grounded on a rock and shivered from stem to stern.

As soon as she struck, it was apparent that the crew would have no difficulty in getting ashore if they had to abandon the ship. There was, however, some danger that her spars might come down and crush some of them on the deck. The ship had been under lower and upper topsail and one staysail when she struck.

The lounges on Bowring's coastal steamers, *Portia* (top) and *Prospero* around 1905. (B.I.S. Centenary Book, 1906)

After the initial shock of striking, the captain ordered the manning of the pumps. They were sounded, and it was apparent that the *Stella* was badly damaged and would soon be a total wreck. The men then quickly gathered up their clothes and personal belongings and in good order left the ship to take shelter on the cliffs that towered above them. The captain was the last man to leave the vessel. Had they run ashore after dark, the mate was sure they might have had some difficulty in landing and perhaps lost some of the crew.

Captain Jones remained in Cuckhold's Cove during the night of January 17, and it was hoped that a tug might tow off the *Stella* when the seas abated. However, she was filled with water when Captain Jones left her, and he did not feel that the hull could be salvaged.

Besides Captain R. Jones, master, the crew consisted of Mate William Martin, Bo'sun Richard Wakeham, Cook John Lamb, and Seamen Thomas Edstrom, Joseph Murphy, P. Lundrigan, Stephen Smolkham, and Hans Jensen.

By a strange coincidence, another ship, the *Corsair*, was lost in the same place on December 5, 1865, again with no loss of life.

In Sight of the Narrows: The Wreck of the Geisha June 6, 1909

On May 12, 1909, the 130-ton schooner *Geisha*, under command of Captain Enos, left Cadiz, Spain for Newfoundland. The ship had a good voyage for the first few days, with favourable winds and calm seas. Then, when they were about 150 miles east of the Grand Banks, they encountered icebergs. On Thursday, June 1, they rammed an iceberg, which carried away the *Geisha's* bowsprit and all her top canvas.

The same night, the *Geisha* ran into another schooner which had no sidelights up. When Captain Enos called out to know the name of the ship, a voice answered, "the *William Bearns*." It was later discovered that there was no such ship in either the Newfoundland coastal or foreign trade. Captain Enos thought that

William Bearns might be the captain's name and not that of the ship. After the impact, the other ship drew away, and Captain Enos and his crew saw no more of her and believed she had gone on her way.

After these two accidents, the voyage proceeded smoothly until around 10:30 P.M., when they were about two miles to the east of Cape Spear. There was a large iceberg in the immediate area, and the tide began to carry the *Geisha* towards it. There was nothing that Captain Enos and his crew could do but stand and watch their ship get carried closer to the berg. When it became evident to all hands that a collision with the iceberg was unavoidable, Captain Enos ordered his men to take to the lifeboats.

They had only rowed about fifty metres from the ship when she struck the iceberg. The berg immediately tumbled over and sank the *Geisha*. It was good seamanship on Captain Enos's part that he had seen the danger in time to save his crew. With the ship gone, the crew manned the oars and began to row towards the Narrows. They had only rowed about half the distance when a passing schooner, the *Jessie B*, took them on board. The *Jessie B* was commanded by Captain Parsons of Greenspond, and they reached St. John's at about 7:00 A.M. The captain and crew had to take to the lifeboat so suddenly, they did not even have time to get their clothes. This loss was keenly felt by the crew members who lost all their personal belongings. The captain and crew were all Englishmen, with the sole exception of one crew member, who was from Trinity, Newfoundland.

The *Geisha* had been built at Appledore in 1906 for R. Cook and Sons, who employed her in the foreign trade.

A Freshwater Bay Shipwreck: The Wreck of the Souris Bell June 2, 1909

On the evening of June 1, 1909, the *Souris Bell*, a forty-four-ton schooner from Western Bay, under the command of Captain Joseph Bishop, was just outside the harbour of St. John's. They had left Western Bay around 4:00 P.M. and after a quick voyage arrived off the Narrows around 8:00 P.M. They had encountered no ice outside Cape Spear, but there was ice in the Narrows and Freshwater Bay.

They attempted to enter St. John's Harbour, but the schooner got caught in ice in the mouth of the Narrows, and around 9:00 P.M. the wind increased from the north-northwest and blew the schooner back out to Freshwater Bay.

With the seas running high on the shoals and the ice and the waves driving the schooner towards the rocks, their situation didn't look too good. However, by dropping their anchors, they managed to slow the drift of the schooner towards destruction and held on until morning.

Around 4:00 A.M., the *Souris Bell* began to drift and drag her anchors. When they got close enough in that it looked like the vessel was going to heel over, the skipper gave the order to launch two lifeboats and see if they could get to land over the broken ice all around them. However, they had only just launched the two boats when a big sea capsized them, throwing the occupants in the water. At the same time, it hove the *Souris Bell* on her beam end.

When the boats overturned, a man named Kennedy and a boy named Whelan scrambled on a large pan of ice; they watched as the ice and sea crushed their lifeboat to splinters

Sailing ships on the premises of Baird, Gordon & Co., circa 1910. (St. John's City Archives)

where they had been standing. The large boat turned bottom-up on the ice, and the men had to jump on the pans to save their lives. The boat was not stove in, however, and six men scrambled to her and got aboard in safety. The boat was still in danger, for it was feared that with the heavy tide and sea the two ice pans might come together and crush the boat like an eggshell.

They also saw Kennedy and Whelan on an ice pan about a gunshot away from them, and in response to their cries for help made an attempt to take them off. They threw a rope, but it fell short of the men on the ice pan. Then, the swell broke again and threatened to dash their boat to pieces. It would mean sacrificing their own lives to stay longer, so they set out for shore, leaving Kennedy and Whelan stranded on a small pan of ice about six feet by twelve feet.

It was hard going for the men in the boat, for when the ice came together, they would have to jump on the ice and pull the boat along, then when the ice separated, they jumped in the boat and continued rowing. It was tough going, and their legs and arms were cut by the ice before they finally reached Petty Harbour and were taken in and cared for by the citizens of that community.

In the meantime, Kennedy and Whelan were drifting in towards the rocks at Cape Spear with the waves washing over their small ice pan, sometimes as high their knees. They saw the *Souris Bell* turn over, go bottom-up, and sink. It was then the boy Whelan almost gave up hope and was going to lie down on the ice and die. Kennedy encouraged him to hang on just a little longer. He kept telling him they would be seen from the Cape Spear lighthouse, and the keeper would telephone for a tug to come and assist them. Then, at about 8:00 P.M., the steam tug *Ingraham* appeared out of the fog and rescued them. Kennedy had been right: the lightkeeper had seen them and telephoned for help. After two hours of staring death in the face, they were finally safe.

On landing, both men went to the store of Mr. Jesse Whiteway and were supplied with dry clothing. The *Souris Bell* was insured, but the crew lost everything.

Sunk in the Narrows: The Loss of the Phoebe November 13, 1909

On the morning of November 13, 1909, the schooner *Phoebe*, under the command of R. J. Strange, left St. John's for Random Sound. The schooner was in ballast, and counting the captain carried a crew of four. As the wind was unfavourable, the vessel was trying to beat out the Narrows in the teeth of a gale. On one tack, she miscarried because of the high winds and ran into a little cove known as Pilot's Cove, under Fort Amherst.

There was a terrific sea running at the time, and as sea after sea swept into the cove, the vessel was slammed against the rocks. Captain Strange and his crew had great difficulty in launching a boat, which was their only hope of survival. They got into the boat with great difficulty, for the raging seas threatened to capsize her, but they got away from the schooner. A few minutes after they had left the ship, she was pounded to pieces on the rocks, and had they stayed with the ship they would all have been drowned.

After a hard struggle, they managed to land near Fort Amherst and made their way up to the lighthouse, where they were well looked after. The schooner was insured for $700.00, but no insurance was carried on the crew's personal effects, all of which were lost in the wreck. A quantity of fishing gear was also lost.

The Wreck of the SS Marsland July 2, 1933

Around 5:30 A.M. on July 2, the SS *Marsland*, on a voyage from Cadiz with 7,000 tons of salt, was being piloted through the Narrows by Pilot Malone. In an effort to avoid a collision with a knockabout schooner beating in the Narrows, he headed the steamer into Hay Cove on the northern side, where she grounded. She then went astern and backed on Vestal Rock. Robert Sheppard, who had just extinguished the light at Fort Amherst, heard the whistle of the *Marsland*, and going to his window he saw that the steamer was aground. He telephoned the Honourable J. G. Stone, the Minister of Marine and Fisheries, and reported the grounding. Mr. Stone immediately arranged for two tugs to go to the aid of the steamer.

It was half-tide when the vessel struck, and there is only about three fathoms of water on the rock at low tide. The rock tore three holes in the ship's bottom, and she began to fill with water.

At 6:30 A.M., the tug *Hugh D* arrived, followed shortly after by the tug *Mouton*. The Canadian hospital ship *Arras* arrived an hour later. The *Arras* and both tugs put lines aboard the *Marsland* and pulled in a northeast direction for about fifteen minutes, until the tow lines parted. For the rest of the morning, the tugs tried to free the grounded ship, but all to no avail. The *Mouton* then took the crews' clothes and came back in the harbour. The *Hugh D* stayed alongside the *Marsland*, and the captain and crew remained on the ship. The news of the grounding spread rapidly, and soon hundreds of people were on their way to Fort Amherst to view the scene.

The SS Marsland. *(Courtesy of Captain Tom Goodyear)*

The attempts to tow the ship off the rock having failed, it was decided to jettison cargo in an effort to lighten her, in the hope she could be pulled off at high tide. The crew took off the hatches, and the derricks began to remove the salt.

The next morning, July 3, the SS *Meigle* arrived with special pumps which were set up, and the water entering the ship was kept in check. As well, Bowring Brothers, the agents for Lloyds of London, hired a number of workmen to discharge her cargo, and schooners and boats in the harbour came alongside to get as much of the free salt as they could. Crowds of people from St. John's were on Signal Hill and other vantage points to view the operation.

In the forenoon of July 3, when much of her cargo had been unloaded, another attempt was made to refloat the steamer. This time, the SS *Meigle*, assisted by the SS *Argyle*, tried to tow her off, but again the hawsers broke. When the tide was high, the *Argyle* and *Meigle*, assisted by the SS *Nova Scotia*, again tried to tow her off. This attempt also failed.

On July 8, the tug *Foundation Franklyn* arrived, and more pumps were put aboard the *Marsland*, whose starboard rail and part of her midships deck were now being washed by the waves. From their vantage points on the surrounding hills, men wagered how long it would take to refloat the *Marsland*. But the *Foundation Franklyn* also failed to move the stranded steamer.

On July 24, the *Marsland* was stripped by the crew of the *Foundation Franklyn*, and there was some looting. This created a rumour which ran through the city, that a visiting British warship, HMS *Norfolk*, was going to blow up the wreck. However, this proved to be unnecessary, for in a few days the wreck of the *Marsland* slipped off the rock and disappeared beneath the sea.

On July 11, 1933, the members of the St. John's Harbour Pilotage met in the office of the Minister of Marine & Fisheries to inquire into the causes of the stranding of the SS *Marsland*.

They heard testimony from the chief officers of the *Marsland* and the helmsman, as well as from the pilot, Edward Malone.

On July 25, 1933, the members of the St. John's Pilotage Commission met again and this time made the following recommendation regarding the pilot, Edward Malone:

> We accordingly recommend that the pilot's certificate or license of Edward Malone be suspended for one year from the date of the stranding of the SS *Marsland*, namely, July 2, 1933.

However, the matter did not end there, for the Department of the Secretary of State, under the Honourable John C. Puddester, later Sir John Puddester, now intervened. His department asked that the commission withdraw their recommendation of July 25, suggesting the suspension of Mr. Malone's Pilot's license for one year. In its place, they asked that a new recommendation, calling for the dismissal of Mr. Malone, be forwarded to the Secretary of State.

The commission bowed to the wishes of the Honourable John Puddester's Department, withdrew their first recommendation, and recommended instead that Mr. Malone be dismissed.

Portuguese White Fleet, circa 1960. (St. John's City Archives)

Shea's Wharf, later known as Harvey and Company, Pier 2. It was situated at the bottom of Cochrane Street opposite the Water Street entrance of the Sir Humphrey Gilbert Building. The steamship is one of the Allan Line for which Sir Ambrose Shea was the Newfoundland Agent. (Courtesy of the Newfoundland Provincial Archives)

Section VI

The Ghosts and Haunted Places of St. John's

A GHOSTLY APPARITION. (LONDON ILLUSTRATED NEWS, 1882)

The Ghosts and Haunted Places on the St. John's Waterfront

For five centuries, the seaport of St. John's has seen the arrival and departure of ships of many nations. With such a long history, there have, of course, been numerous stories of ghost ships, haunted buildings, and ghostly sightings along the St. John's waterfront.

Ghostly sightings were most frequent in the spring and fall, when, under cover of the grey mists that creep in from the sea, ghostly ships from bygone days returned to St. John's Harbour. Ancient galleons, warships, barques, brigs, and topsail schooners paid their nocturnal visits. Two salt hulks, one of them the former HMS *Calypso* (renamed HMS *Britton*), were moored in St. John's Harbour for many years. Although they had been stripped of everything, people on the docks after midnight would sometimes hear the ships' bells ring out the hours, and ghostly longboats could be seen approaching the hulks. The occupants in the boats dressed in old naval uniforms, approached the ship from the port side, and came to rest navy-style, with their oars up.

Another common sighting in late spring was that of the ill-fated *Southern Cross*, which was lost with all hands in 1914. She would steam through the Narrows with her flags flying and crew assembled on the deck, sail up the harbour, and then disappear.

In the early 1920s, one group of men waiting for the arrival of a vessel to load salt for Change Islands at the Gordon Pew premises on the Southside had an eerie experience. The steamer was due around midnight, and the loading crew were awaiting her arrival, when a small two-masted schooner with no lights suddenly appeared and began to dock.

The men watched as the ship manoeuvred into the wharf, not fifty metres from where they were standing. The strange thing was that there were no persons visible on the schooner, there was no sound of an engine, and the ship's sails were furled.

As the amazed longshoremen watched, the doors of a nearby shed opened, and about twenty barrels and tierces were rolled out by invisible hands. Then the hatches on the schooner were opened, they heard the clink of a chain, and the cargo was stored in the hold of the schooner. When the last barrels had been hoisted aboard, the hatches were replaced, and the ghost ship moved away from the dock and sailed out the Narrows.

Another story is told of an immense, black ghost barque that is seen in St. John's Harbour and is always an omen of a forthcoming disaster. This vessel can always be identified by her large size and her gargoyle figurehead. When the *Desola* caught fire and burned off C. F. Bennett's wharf, the huge black barque was seen lying nearby, clearly outlined in the glow of the burning hull of the *Desola*. She was seen just before the fire of 1892, and again in 1914 when the crew of the SS *Newfoundland* were stranded on the ice and the *Southern Cross* went down. A number of people saw her clearly on the eve of the July Drive, which brought sorrow to so many Newfoundland homes. During World War II, her appearance signalled some naval disaster.

There is also an interesting ghost story about the SS *Yankton*, a converted yacht once owned by Sarah Bernhardt. She arrived in St. John's on December 27, 1923, and it was rumoured that a fireman on the ship told her captain that he had seen a strange man board their ship as they passed the *Sambro Lightship* on their way to St. John's. Later, as the ship was passing Cape Race, the helmsman and third mate reported seeing a face peering at them through the bridge portholes. The ghostly figure left the ship on her arrival in St. John's, and it was said by the men on the dock that the strange man was the ghost of some drowned sailor who wanted to return home. Hickman's coal shed in the West End and Bowring's wharf were also haunted.

Other Ghosts and Haunted Places

Friendly Hall on Robinson's Hill was supposed to be haunted, and few cared to linger in its vicinity after dark. Bennett's Grove on Forest Road was supposed to be haunted by Captain Kidd and his pirate crew. Deadman's Pond on Signal Hill is haunted by a pirate who was killed there to guard a buried treasure.

Restless spirits haunted two houses on Queen's Road and another on Mullock Street. There were ghosts at the old Parade Rink, and one near Rennie's Bridge, which was believed to be that of Ensign John Philpot, who was killed in a duel nearby. A house on Bannerman Street was said to be troubled by the spirit of a white horse that galloped up a stairway and then vanished through a second-storey window. A house on Circular Road was haunted by the spirit of a soldier killed in the July Drive, and no one could live in it without encountering the ghost.

On Duckworth Street, the ghost of Catherine Snow is often seen. Mrs Snow was hanged from the west window of the old courthouse on Duckworth Street for conspiring with two men, T. Mandeville and Arthur Spring, to kill her husband. She went to the gallows protesting her innocence. In fact, the priest who attended her on the night before her hanging was so convinced of her innocence he started a petition, asking the Governor for a new trial. He collected a huge number of signatures, but the Governor paid no attention to the petition, and the hanging took place. On February 15, 1890, the local papers reported that officers at the courthouse said they saw a ghost there.

In all parts of the city, the fearsome "dead car" was often seen or heard rumbling along, and to meet with it was a sign of an impending death in the family.

In later years, there have been reports of ghosts at Gonzaga High School, St. Patrick's Church on Patrick Street, St. Clare's Hospital, and the old Belvedere Orphanage building.

On Brookfield Road, the ghost of Lady James Pearl is often seen, especially in August. She rides out from the farm on a white horse and gallops away towards Bowring Park.

A haunted house. (*London Illustrated News*)

The Ghost of Casey's Lane

In 1907, the Boys of Casey's Lane in the West End of St. John's were celebrated in a rhyme that was published in the *Evening Chronicle*:

We are the boys from Casey's Lane
At night time we have fun,
For when a policeman shows his nose
Up Flower's Hill we run.
We stand behind the coffin house
We don't know snow or rain,
There's none koopup a corner,
Like the boys from Casey's Lane.

Around the turn of the nineteenth century, one of the boys from Casey's Lane came back from the dead to fulfill a vow taken on his wedding night to claim his bride if he died at sea. His name was Matt Trilligan.

Matt Trilligan grew up in a house on Casey's Lane. He was a devil-may-care fellow who feared nothing or no one. At an early age, he went to sea, and by the time he had reached manhood had seen many strange cities and weathered many a storm. Europe, the West Indies, and Brazil were all familiar places to the seafarer. At times, he was absent from St. John's for several years at a time and often given up for lost, but like the bad penny, he always returned. Like most young sailors of his time, he had "a great thirst," and during his short stays on shore found congenial company in the rum shops that dotted the St. John's waterfront.

Then, he fell madly in love with a young girl named Kathleen, whom he had met at a family gathering. She too was smitten with his charms, and in a very short while they were walking out together. Of course Matt still had to go to sea, but now his voyages were shorter, and he was always anxious to get back to St. John's. After some time, the two became engaged, and a date was set for a spring wedding. In the meantime, Matt brought Kathleen back many gifts from such far away places as Oporto, Rio, and the Indies.

At last, the wedding date arrived, and Matt Trilligan and his bride were united in marriage. A wedding supper was held at the home of the bride, and family members and old friends were invited to help celebrate the wedding. As was the custom in those days, the house was thrown open to the guests, and in true Newfoundland fashion, the ladies gathered with the bride in one room, sipping sherry or gin and exchanging stories that were calculated to chill the blood of the new bride, while in a separate room, the men tossed off large glasses of dark rum and spoke of storms and winds and tides and ice floes.

Matt Trilligan, having drunk to the health of his bride a number of times and listened to the oft-repeated tales of great voyages and bumper seal catches, wandered out, glass of rum in hand, to the hallway, anxious to catch a glimpse of his new bride. As he stood quietly by the stairpost, staring in unabashed adoration at his loved one in the room across the way, the conversation of the ladies came to him.

One old matron of uncertain years and questionable sobriety was holding forth on what the future held for Kathleen as the wife of a sailor.

"Ah! Me love," she said in a mournful tone, "'tis a hard life it is, to be the wife of a sailor man. Months and months you'll spend alone, waiting and watching, listening to the wind howling in the chimney and tearing at the windows and the whitecaps breaking over the Chain Rock. Then there's the long weary nights alone, wondering and fearing that he'll never come back to you. Seeing in your mind's eye his poor body lying cold and alone on the bottom of the ocean, with never a soul to know his final resting place, and you still waiting and never knowing whether or not you're a widow as the years pass."

She stopped suddenly, for she saw Matt Trilligan, glass in hand, standing in the doorway. He had a strange smile on his face and a look in his eye that made the old women shiver. He came into the room, went to his bride, threw his arm about her shoulder, and then he spoke.

"Now, never you fear, my darling Kathleen, 'twill never be that way for you. I, Matt Trilligan, your husband, swear it."

He stopped and looked around the room, and his glance fell on a large crucifix hanging on the wall. He reached up, took down the crucifix, and the ladies in the room felt a shiver of fear go through their bodies. Laying his glass on a table, he held the crucifix in his left hand and laid his right hand across the figure nailed to the cross. Then, in a slow and almost mocking voice, he said, "I swear to you, Kathleen, my bride, that if ever death shall come for Matt Trilligan, you will be the first to know. For whether it be to Heaven or to Hell I must go, I will come for you and take you with me, and this I swear with my hand upon this crucifix." And picking up his glass, he drained it.

The ladies—the bride excepted—were in shock. They crossed themselves and muttered short prayers of protection from the powers of evil. Only Kathleen, the bride, showed no fear, and laying her hand on the crucifix above her husband's, she said, "And if you come for me, I will go freely with you, Matt Trilligan, my husband, to Heaven or to Hell. This I swear on the holy crucifix." And they sealed their death pact with a kiss.

The story of the strange wedding oath was told and retold, with many muttered warnings of dire things to come. However, Trilligan and his new bride only laughed at the horror their strange death pact aroused in all who heard of it. The young couple moved into the Trilligan house on Casey's Lane and seemed to be as happy and devoted to each other as was possible to be. But, eventually, Matt had to go back to sea. Kathleen came down to the wharf to see him off and stayed, watching the big three-masted schooner sail out the harbour, until it disappeared through the Narrows, bound for the Spanish coast.

It would be a long voyage, and young Mrs. Trilligan settled down in the house on Casey's Lane to wait the return of her husband. The days grew into weeks, the weeks into months, other ships returned, but not the one Matt Trilligan had sailed on. There were tidings, though, from other ships, that did return. She had reached Oporto, unloaded her cargo of fish, loaded a cargo of salt, and sailed for home. As October gave way to November, hope for the safe return of Matt Trilligan's ship faded, and even the firm that owned her gave her up for lost. Only Kathleen Trilligan refused to give up hope, saying, "I know that he's not dead, for if he was, he'd have come for me like he promised." It was then that people again recalled the wedding oath and shivered in fear.

Around the middle of November, on a cold, damp evening, with the fog lying over the city, Mrs. Cleary, who lived across the way from the Trilligan house, looked out her front window and saw a familiar figure coming up Casey Street. It was Matt Trilligan, and Mrs. Cleary was delighted at his safe return. She watched him walk slowly up the street towards Casey's Lane, and she ran to her door to welcome him home. But, as he came closer, she realized that there was something unreal about the figure dressed in oilskins, and as he passed under her window, she saw in the reflection of her lamp the deadly pallor of his face and his eyes fixed and unseeing. At the sight of that familiar yet spectral figure walking towards the Trilligan house, a terrible fear came over her, and she could neither speak nor move, but seemed rooted to her doorstep.

Standing there in her doorway, she saw Matt Trilligan enter his house, and the door closed behind him. A few moments passed, and then faintly, from the house across the way, she heard a single cry, and her blood froze in her veins. Moments later, the door of the Trilligan house opened, and Matt Trilligan came out, but not alone, for in his arms he carried his bride, who also seemed more of a spectre than a living person. Down Casey's Lane they went and then disappeared from sight at the point where Casey's Lane met New Gower Street.

As the two forms disappeared into the gathering darkness, Mrs. Cleary felt as if a spell had been lifted from her, and she was herself again. Her first action was to fall to her knees and murmur a prayer for the souls of Matt and Kathleen Trilligan, for she was sure Matt Trilligan had come to fulfill his wedding oath.

A little later, she gathered her courage and went over to the Trilligan house and asked to see Kathleen. She was told that Kathleen was upstairs in her bedroom. They called out to her, but there was no answer. Then one of Matt Trilligan's sisters went upstairs to see if she was asleep. Her scream of terror left no doubt in Mrs. Cleary's mind as to what had happened. She rushed upstairs with the other members of the Trilligan family who were home, and saw a sight that she would never forget. Kathleen Trilligan's lifeless body was lying draped across her bed, with her long, golden hair resting on the floor in a small puddle of water, seaweed, and shells. For Mrs. Cleary, it was proof enough that Matt Trilligan had kept his wedding vow and returned from the dead to claim his bride.

The Haunted Hotel Room

One of the old ghost stories of a St. John's hotel was preserved by Mr. P. J. Kinsella. It concerned a haunted hotel room and the sudden death of a guest in a room at the Foran Hotel, which was situated before the fire of 1892 on the present site of the General Post Office Building on Water Street West. This hotel was the favourite of many travellers from the outports who had to spend a day or two in St. John's.

Late one night, some years before the 1892 fire, when most of the hotel guests had retired, a strange knocking sound was heard coming from a vacant room at the top of the house. The knocking was so loud and persistent that it woke all the guests. There was great commotion in the hotel hallway, with the more timid keeping close together, while a few of the braver raced upstairs to investigate.

They identified the room where the noise was coming from and cautiously entered the top-floor bedroom. As soon as they entered the room, the knocking ceased. The men searched the room very carefully and found nothing to account for the loud knocking. They finally gave up and went back downstairs, and as the noise had stopped, all hands went back to bed.

At exactly the same time the next night, the knocking was heard again, and this time it was even louder. The men went up and made another search of the room, but, as before, nothing was found to account for the noise. The baffled searchers retired as on the previous night, and there was no more knocking. The next night, at the same hour, the knocking began again. This time everyone in the hotel took part in searching the upper floor. They found absolutely nothing that could account for the strange phenomenon.

After the third successive night of disturbances, there were whispers of the place being haunted, and some of the more timid guests began to think of moving to another hotel. The more faithful clientele of the hotel, who didn't wish to see the place lose its good reputation, worked on the other guests to stay just one more night. They promised that if there was any more knocking they would either prove or disprove the presence of a ghost. To do this, one well-known old sea captain organized the hotel's guests and management into watches which would guard the entrance, the hall, and the staircase leading to the upstairs room at all times. To make doubly sure no one entered the room in question, two persons were appointed to stand guard at the door to the noisy bedchamber.

They stood guard all night, but all was quiet in the upper bedroom. When morning came, the old sea captain stated that this proved it wasn't a ghost that made the noise. "Somehow, someone had managed to get in the noisy bedchamber," he said, "make the noise, and then escape before being caught." All hands agreed that it must have been the work of a facetious guest, and the reputation of the hotel was saved.

Everything went well with the hotel until about six months after the knocking incidents. Then, late one evening, a stranger came to the Foran Hotel seeking lodgings. He was taken in and made welcome. However, as the hotel was pretty well full that evening, the stranger was given the top-floor room that had been "troubled" earlier by the strange knocking. As the man was a stranger, the clerk didn't mention anything about the knocking that had emanated from the room six months earlier.

The new guest sat around and talked with the other guests after supper and about 11:00 retired to his room. A few minutes later, the most ungodly racket was heard coming from that room. It was loud and continuous and brought every guest in the hotel to the door of the room that had been troubled.

They tried the bedroom door, and it opened to their touch. They entered the room and saw the figure of the strange guest lying motionless on the bed. He was fully dressed but showed no visible wounds. The hotel doctor was called in, and after examining the corpse, he declared that the man had died of a violent hemorrhage.

The police were called in, and it was discovered the man carried no identification and was a total stranger to everyone in the hotel. The body was left in the room overnight, and the next morning, the undertaker came with a coffin to collect it. As the coffin was being carried out of the room, a sudden, violent knocking filled the room, frightening the undertaker and his men nearly to death. They dropped the coffin and fled downstairs. The noise continued for several minutes, and then, as suddenly as it had begun, the knocking stopped.

After several large glasses of brandy administered by the hotel keeper, the undertaker and his men again ventured upstairs. They picked up the coffin, and when nothing happened, they quickly descended the stairs and took the body away.

The man was later buried in the old cemetery at the foot of Long's Hill, but his identity always remained a mystery. Following the untimely death of the stranger in the "troubled" bedroom, the window and door of that room were nailed shut. It was never used again, and the noisy knocks from the room were heard no more. However, the question of who he was and what connection the strange knocking had that preceding his coming and his death were questions the guests and the staff of the old Foran Hotel were never tired of discussing.

A ghostly funeral. (*London Illustrated News*)

The Ghost of Long Pond Road

In the early part of the eighteenth century, a Captain Bute, who was a senior army officer in St. John's, had a residence at the western end of Long Pond, near what used to be known as the Sand Pits. According to the tradition handed down by the older people, Bute's residence was of palatial proportions and built like a fortress to protect him, should he come under attack. Bute also had a dungeon under his house, which was used to punish his servants and the soldiers who fell under his displeasure.

The captain was fond of liquor and company and gave many parties and balls which were well attended. The drinking and dancing went on all night, and the sounds of the revellers often echoed along Nagle's Hill until daylight was well abroad. A heavy drinker, Captain Bute would be in a state of apathy or semi-stupor for days after one of his parties. In this state, he was so vicious and quarrelsome that none of his servants or the soldiers would dare disturb him.

At one of his parties, a manservant was unfortunate enough to annoy the captain. He immediately flew into a great rage, and after berating his servant dragged him down to the underground dungeon and told him he would stay until he learned proper respect. Following the party at which this incident happened, Captain Bute was in an even more vicious state than usual, and no one dared mention the poor servant confined below the house. He remained there without food or water.

About eight days after the man had been thrown in the dungeon, Captain Bute threw a another party. The wine was flowing freely, and the noise of wild celebration echoed from the surrounding countryside, when a loud groaning which grew and grew in volume echoed from the floor beneath the revellers. So terrible was the groaning that even in his half-drunken state Captain Bute suddenly remembered the servant he had confined to the dungeon eight days previously. His confidence restored that the sounds were coming from the prisoner below, he invited his friends to accompany him down to the dungeon and see the "disobeying dog."

The party made their way down to the dungeon, and when the captain unlocked the iron door, they all crowded into the prison.

However, the sight that met their eyes sobered even the most callous of the group. The servant was dead, and had been for several days. It was then Bute and his friends realized that the groaning they had heard was not from a living man. In great panic, they fled the dungeon and ran upstairs, fearing every moment they would be the victims of an avenging spirit.

As Bute was the sole legal authority in St. John's in the absence of the fishing admiral and naval officer, there was no one to punish him for his cruel deed. However, a little while after, Bute's house burned to the ground in mysterious circumstances, and the captain left Newfoundland.

The clearing where the house stood and the foundation stones were visible for many years, but few people cared to pass that spot after dark. Those who did testified that they heard terrible groaning sounds coming from beneath the foundation, and the spot was "troubled" by ghostly apparitions for many years.

A Haunted House on the Shores of Quidi Vidi Lake

On the morning of June 17, 1801, the citizens of St. John's discovered the following placard posted on buildings in various conspicuous parts of the town:

> DESERTED!
>
> Whereas, two seamen of HMS *Sphynx*, presently in port, have deserted, and are believed to be hiding somewhere in the town of St. John's, and whereas there is a law on the Statutes expressly prohibiting the harbouring of a seaman, I hereby notify all whom it may concern that the person harbouring the above, if proven guilty, will be fined 10 pounds for each seaman; furthermore a suitable reward will be given to any person or persons who will give such information as will lead to the arrest of the men.
>
> Signed, Jonathan Ogden, J.P.

The people of St. John's knew that the marines from the *Sphynx* had full authority to search any house in the town, and it was felt the men would be captured. Howcvcr, the searches did not turn up the men, and a week later the news of a murder in a house on the shores of Quidi Vidi Lake in an area called The Forest occupied everyone's interest.

The house in the Forest was owned by Samuel Bingwell, a wealthy retired planter who lived there with a niece named

Rosanna Perks and a housekeeper. On June 27, Miss Perks came to town and gave the magistrates the details of the murder.

On the night of June 26, about 10:15 P.M., when Mr. Bingwell and his family were preparing to retire, there came a loud knocking on the door. As her uncle was upstairs, Roseanna answered the door. She found two marines, who apologized for the lateness of their visit, but said they were searching for the two deserters. She called out to her uncle that the two marines wanted to search their house, and he told her to send them up to him.

When the two marines went upstairs, Roseanna went into the parlour and stayed there until she heard the two men coming down the stairs. They told her they had completed their search, apologized for disturbing the family, and she let them out. She remained in the parlour for about ten minutes, expecting her uncle to come down, and wondering what was delaying him. When she heard no sound from her uncle's room, she went up to investigate.

She knocked on his bedroom door, and when there was no answer, she opened it and found her uncle on the floor, lying on his back in a pool of blood. Unnerved by the ghastly sight, she screamed and then fainted. The housekeeper came to the room and revived her, and then the two women ran out of the house, screaming murder. Alarmed by the women's screams, a crowd gathered and accompanied the women back to the house in the Forest. On examination, the uncle was pronounced dead. As well, his strongbox, which was lying next to him, and which had contained a large number of Bank of England notes and golden guineas, was now empty.

The authorities now took charge of the case, and a search was made for the two marines. The police suspected the two murderers were members of the crew of the HMS *Sphynx* and brought Roseanna aboard the warship in the hopes of identifying the culprits. The ship's crew were paraded before her, but she did not find either of the two marines who had murdered her uncle.

The investigation continued, and a large reward was posted for information leading to the whereabouts of the two wanted men, but no one came forward. After a time, interest in the case dwindled, and Roseanna, after residing with some distant relatives in St. John's for a while, went to the United States. After her departure, stories were told of strange flickering lights being seen in the old house, and occasionally some traveller would see the ghostly figure of an old man sitting on a bench near the main entrance. When these stories were spread abroad, people began to give the house a wide berth, and the house became known as the Haunted House in the Forest.

Then, some ten years later, people were surprised when Miss Perks reappeared with a daughter and opened up her uncle's house. After a time, she revealed a very strange story concerning her Uncle's murderer.

She had gone to Salem, Massachusetts, and there she met Philip le Magor, a Salem businessman who operated a billiards parlour. In time, she fell in love and married him, and they had one daughter whom they named Rose. Philip proved to be a good husband and a caring father. Neither Roseanna or her husband discussed their lives before their marriage, and both knew little of each other's past.

About eight years after their marriage, Roseanna received a letter from one of her St. John's relatives. In the letter, the writer made some reference to her murdered uncle, and the mention of the terrible deed brought the memory of it back, and Roseanna began to weep. Her husband tried to comfort her, and she broke down and told him of that terrible night in the house in the Forest.

Her husband was greatly agitated by this revelation, and for the next few days he was moody and seemed to have something on his mind. A week later, he told his wife he had to go to Boston on business and would be away for a few days. Before leaving, he told his wife that if anything happened to him she would find his will and private papers in a tin box at the bottom of the bookcase.

Two days later, Roseanna received word that her husband had fallen to his death from a window in the Boston hotel where he was staying. It was believed he had walked in his sleep and fallen through the open window. When she recovered from the shock of her husband's death, Roseanna went to the bookcase and took out the tin box with the will and private papers.

When she examined the papers, she discovered to her horror that her husband, Philip le Magor, had been one of the men involved in her uncle's murder. He had not struck the fatal blow but had been party to the robbery. Philip and his companion had been crew members on a Jersey brig in St. John's Harbour at the time the sailors deserted from the *Sphynx*. They had heard that Bingwell kept a large sum of money in his house and seized the opportunity to go under the guise of searching for the deserters to rob him.

Following the robbery, they returned to their ship, hid their ill-gotten gold, and got safely out of the country. Philip's accomplice died soon after, and Philip came in for the whole of it. However, Philip's conscience bothered him, and he put the money away, with the idea he would one day return it to its rightful owner.

The box also contained Bingwell's will, which, besides leaving everything he owned to Roseanna, also asked that she always continue to live in the house in the Forest. When she recovered from the shock of her husband's death and the subsequent discovery that he had been involved in her uncle's death, she sold off her possessions in Salem and returned to St. John's with her little daughter.

Her return seemed to satisfy old Bingwell's ghost, for after she took up residence in the old house, the ghostly figure of the old man and the flickering lights were never seen again. Roseanna married again a few years later and lived out her days on the shores of Quidi Vidi Lake.

Section VII

Highlights of the Mayors of St. John's

St. John's City Hall, early 1960s. (St. John's City Archives)

First Municipal Act

It was through the efforts of Sir Robert Thorburn, Prime Minister from 1885-1889, that the first municipal government in the then colony was initiated by the passage of the Municipal Act (51 Vic., C.5), which gave St. John's a seven-member council, two members being appointed by the government of the day. In 1888, five wards encompassed specific streets and roads, and the people living in these wards voted only for the candidate in their particular area. One of the major concerns of the citizens of St. John's at the time the city was incorporated was the provision of an adequate water supply for personal needs and protection against fire, which in a town of wooden buildings could destroy the entire community, as had happened in 1846. The Great Fire of 1892 proved these fears to be justified.

The Municipal Act of 1888 placed a number of conditions on the first city council. The Legislature of the colony demanded an annual balanced statement of revenues and expenditures. Furthermore, the council was seen as a creature of the Colonial Government. To ensure that property owners would not be excessively taxed—thereby jeopardizing the chances of the St. John's members of the Legislature being re-elected—the council was obliged to receive approval of the Legislature before increasing local property taxes.

First Municipal Election

The first election under Thorburn's Municipal Act was held on August 30, 1888, it being the first election in Newfoundland, we are told, where the secret ballot was used in voting. It was a patriarchal age where only the male resident who had paid fees to the General Water Company could vote. The following candidates were elected from the five wards: John Carnell, Ward 1; Francis St. John, Ward 2; Moses Monroe, Ward 3; Michael Power, Ward 4; William Morrison, Ward 5. The two government appointees were James Fox and James Goodfellow, who was appointed chairman.

The newly established council held its first meeting on September 28, 1888 in the Keough Estate Building on Duckworth Street. This council held office until January 23, 1892, when a second election saw the following in office: John Carnell, Ward 1; John Southcott, Jr., Ward 2; James Goodfellow, Ward 3; Michael Power, Ward 4; Donald Morrison, Ward 5. Edward Bennett and Thomas Mitchell were the government appointees, with the latter serving as chairman.

The third municipal election was held on January 23, 1896, resulting in the following being elected: John Harris, Ward 1; Thomas Keating, Ward 2; John V. O'Dea, Ward 3; Michael Power, Ward 4; James Callahan, Ward 5. Thomas Edens and R. A. McCoubrey were appointed by the government, with Michael Power being elected chairman at the first meeting. During this year, the office of Secretary-Treasurer was established with the appointment of P. W. Kelly to the position. He held office from 1895 to 1899. The council was abolished in 1898 and replaced by an appointed commission. Councils from 1888 to 1898 became embroiled in a number of partisan issues pertaining to the Whiteway, Goodridge, Winter and Bond administrations of the Newfoundland Government.

It was the great Prime Minister, statesman and diplomat Sir Robert Bond who had legislation passed that gave St. John's a city council consisting of a mayor and six councillors elected at large for which all men (women did not then have the franchise) twenty-one and over could vote.

First Mayor of St. John's

George Edward Shea was born in St. John's on July 4, 1851, the son of a very prominent politician, Sir Edward Dalton Shea, and nephew of the famous Father of Confederation and Governor of the Bahamas, Sir Ambrose Shea. George Shea had represented the District of Ferryland for the Liberal Party in 1886 and succeeded his uncle, Sir Ambrose Shea, as managing partner of Shea and Company, Newfoundland agents for the Allan Line of Royal Mail Steamships. He was also very active in the cultural and business life of St. John's.

George Shea's tenure as Mayor was characterized by sound financial management resulting in part from a windfall settlement of $250,000 paid to the council on May 4, 1904, for land which the former Winter administration had given to the Reid Newfoundland Company in 1898. The council of the day proposed increases in taxes, the coal duty and sewage rates which were approved by the Legislature. Shea's term was notable for improvements in the water system and the establishment of a permanent medical health officer for St. John's. Shea contested the June 26, 1906 election and lost to well-known lawyer and union activist Michael P. Gibbs. He continued to be active in the politics of the colony, serving as Minister Without Portfolio in Sir Robert Bond's government from 1904-1909, and he was re-elected in 1908 and 1909. After retiring from business, he was appointed by Sir Richard Anderson Squires to the Legislative Council. He passed away on September 13, 1932.

The Second Mayor

Michael P. Gibbs was born in St. John's on March 25, 1870. He became a well-known lawyer, politician, unionist and social activist who had been elected for the Conservatives in the District of St. Georges in 1897 and quickly earned respect and esteem as a reformer. He was the editor of the *Terra Nova Advocate* in 1893 and will be remembered by labour historians for organizing the Longshoremen's Protective Union.

Gibbs also organized the bakers and carpenters in St. John's, and his prominence as a union lawyer no doubt was instrumen-

George Shea
1902-1906
(Archives of St. John's City Hall)

Michael P. Gibbs
1906-1910
(Archives of St. John's City Hall)

Mayors of St. John's 1902-1921

William J. Ellis
1910-1914
(Archives of St. John's City Hall)

William G. Gosling
1914-1921
(Archives of St. John's City Hall)

tal in getting him elected as Mayor in 1906. One of the ironies of the Gibbs administration was that while a union activist was in power, St. John's had its first civic strike when the sanitary workers protested the suspension of a number of their members.

Highlights of Gibbs's term as Mayor included the passage of legislation to connect water and sewerage to the homes of the St. John's working class, the passing of the 1910 Municipal Act regulating the height and location of various buildings, and the prevention of pollution of the Windsor Lake water supply.

Gibbs was instrumental in providing fire escapes and washroom facilities in factories and other places of work. The working man's mayor did not run for re-election on June 27, 1910 and was succeeded by Councillor William J. Ellis, who was unopposed and won the mayor's seat by acclamation. Gibbs was appointed president of the Legislative Council in 1930 and served in this position until its abolition in 1934, with the advent of Commission of Government. He died in St. John's on November 7, 1943.

The Third Mayor

The 1910 municipal election was uneventful due to the mayor's position being uncontested. William J. Ellis was born in St. John's on July 9, 1857 and became a successful businessman and politician. His reputation rose as a builder and contractor, and he was responsible for restoring such well-known St. John's landmarks as the Roman Catholic Basilica, King George V Institute, and St. Patrick's Roman Catholic Church in the West End of St. John's.

Actively involved in politics, he was first elected to the city council in 1902. In 1904, he was elected as Liberal member of the Legislature for Ferryland district. He was again elected councillor in 1906 and re-elected to the Legislature for Ferryland in 1908. Some highlights of Ellis's tenure as Mayor were the designation of St. John's first official "Cleanup Day" on May 15, 1911, the opening of the first real home of the city council in the former Seaman's Home on Duckworth Street on August 9, 1911, and the acquisition of Bowring Park, a large parcel of land located in the Waterford Valley as a gift to the city from the Bowring family, whose business Bowring Brothers Ltd. had been established in the city in 1811.

Ellis would serve one term as Mayor before the elected form of municipal government was replaced by a commission. He continued to serve as a commissioner in 1914. He was active in politics of the colony, associating himself with such notables as Robert Bond, Edward P. Morris, and William F. Lloyd.

Ellis served in the Legislative Council. He died in New York on April 17, 1926.

The Commission Era

St. John's enjoyed an elected municipal council until July 1, 1914, when William Gilbert Gosling, a very prominent businessman, politician and historian, was instrumental in having the elective form of city government replaced by a commission. Gosling was born in Bermuda on September 8, 1863. It was through his efforts as founder and president of the St. John's Board of Trade that a lobbying citizens' committee concerned with a number of pressing civic matters petitioned the Legislature to have the municipal council suspended and replaced by a municipal board.

The Governor-in-Council appointed a twelve-man commission to administer the city, and they were asked to draft a new Municipal Act. Among those appointed were Gosling and former Mayor Ellis, and at a meeting of the commission held on July 2, 1914 a dispute arose whereby Ellis stated he accepted a position on the commission with the understanding from Prime Minister Edward Morris that he would be chairman due to his experience as councillor and mayor. However, Gosling moved that the chairman be elected by a vote among the twelve and was elected himself. Ellis subsequently resigned with a tinge of bitterness.

Gosling, in his term as chairman of the commission, was frustrated in his efforts to have a new Municipal Act or charter for the city pass the House of Assembly. Because of public wrangling, the life of the Municipal Commission was extended by the Legislature for a further two years, and the House finally passed legislation in 1916 to provide for a return to elected municipal government.

The election was to be held in June, and the councillors were to hold office for two years with the same elected structure as before 1914, but a plebiscite was held whereby the citizens opted for election at large rather than the ward system. Gosling contested the June 19, 1916 election and defeated his only opponent, W. A. O'D Kelly. On January 20, 1920, Gosling requested Sir Richard Squires to pass the municipal charter. It was passed at that year's session of the Legislature, with the municipal election being postponed to give the Legislative Council more time to study the proposed charter.

New Charter Received

The historic moment arrived on August 2, 1921, when the new charter passed the Legislature and Legislative Council. A separate Act of the Legislature established a new Commission of Civic Government to govern the city until a new election was held on December 15, 1921. Gosling refused a place on the commission, resulting in Isaac Morris being appointed the new chairman.

It was a red-letter day for St. John's as the long-awaited 1921 Municipal Act recognized it as a city. It gave the city council authority to raise loans for different municipal projects and permission to establish a sinking fund to repay future loans; it imposed an annual poll tax of five dollars on all men twenty-five and over who did not pay the city tax. Another highlight was the provision made for persons entering into property leases to purchase freehold title to the land.

Public health was a matter dear to the heart of Gosling, and the Act gave permission for council to use its monies to help provide medical service to newborns and sick children, and also to provide free medical examinations for schoolchildren. Some of Gosling's dreams of housing, water, sanitation and public health were fulfilled, and in 1928 he retired from municipal politics and returned to Bermuda where he died on November 5, 1930. His era as Mayor represents one of the more interesting and controversial developments of municipal government in the history of St. John's.

Tasker Cook
1921-1929
(Archives of St. John's City Hall)

Charles J. Howlett
1930-1932
(Archives of St. John's City Hall)

Mayors of St. John's
1921-1965

Andrew G. Carnell
1933-1949
(Archives of St. John's City Hall)

Henry G. R. Mews
1949-1965
(Archives of St. John's City Hall)

Women Get Right to Run

The December 15, 1921 municipal election gave every male British subject twenty-one years of age who was a householder or paid taxes the right to vote. There was still inequality, however, for women. While they could vote, they could not run on the basis that they were ineligible to vote in a colonial election in Newfoundland. Tasker Cook and Isaac Morris contested the mayor's seat, with Cook being victorious. Mayor Cook was born in St. John's on September 25, 1867 and was a leading businessman and politician. He worked in his father's business and in 1907 was appointed Vice-Consul for Norway and later acted as consul for France and Denmark. Some of the highlights of his first term in office were the replacement of the wooden Gull Pond Dam at Windsor Lake with a concrete structure, the water main on Portugal Cove Road was relaid, and LeMarchant Road was widened. He made significant improvements in administering and enhancing Bowring Park. Cook also became known for fiscal responsibility and a businesslike approach to City Hall, and on December 8, 1925 he was elected Mayor by acclamation.

One of the highlights of the 1925 municipal election was the right given to women to run for council for the first time. The women's rights activist Julia Salter Earle came within eleven votes of winning a seat on council. She was born in St. John's on September 20, 1877 and worked for thirty-five years as an engrossing clerk in the House of Assembly, preparing final drafts of legislation. She died on December 9, 1945.

Some of the highlights of Cook's second term as Mayor were the expansion of the Windsor Lake watershed to include Round Pond, construction of the concrete Rennie's Mill and Long bridges, and the installation of concrete steps from Duckworth Street to Water Street.

One of his landmarks as Mayor was the appointment of the city's first Town Planning Commission on April 28, 1928. The commission's mandate was to study all lands and roads within the city and one mile outside, and to report back to council with suggestions for new streets, playgrounds and building lots, to name but a few.

Sir Tasker Cook's political career came to an end in the December 9, 1929 municipal election when he was defeated in his third bid for office by Dr. Charles J. Howlett. Upon his departure from municipal politics, Cook served in the Legislative Council during the Squires administration from 1928 to 1932 and served as chairman of the Railway Commission. He died in St. John's on September 25, 1937.

City's First Bond Issue

Dr. Charles Howlett, politician and dental surgeon, was born in St. John's on January 25, 1885. He defeated Tasker Cook in the race for Mayor by waging an anti-Liberal campaign against the party to which Cook was so closely allied.

Howlett ran St. John's on a sound business and financial basis and obtained the services of a firm of chartered accountants to study and make recommendations for the city. It was through his representation to Sir Richard Squires that the annual grants from the House of Assembly for the districts of St. John's East and West were passed over to the city rather than to the representatives in the Legislature.

Duckworth and New Gower streets were paved during his term. In 1932, the city floated its first bond issue of $500,000 after receiving permission from the Legislature. Newfoundland was experiencing very difficult financial and social conditions during the '30s, and the plight of the poor in St. John's was desperate. Howlett's social conscience led him to organize a Civic Relief Committee to raise money for the poor and destitute. His term as Mayor was short-lived, for he died on March 31, 1932.

Andrew G. Carnell: Cars-Buses-Housing

Andy Carnell was born in St. John's on April 10, 1877 and assumed the position of Acting Mayor upon the death of Mayor Howlett. He was a shrewd businessman, having entered his father's carriage and undertaking business and eventually becoming owner of Carnell's Carriage Factory and Funeral Home. He had made two unsuccessful bids for the Legislature, being defeated as a Liberal candidate for Fortune Bay district in 1908 and for Trinity Bay in 1919 before entering municipal politics on December 9, 1929.

Carnell was elected Mayor by acclamation in the 1933 municipal election. Following the abolition of Responsible Government and the establishment of Commission of Government in Newfoundland in 1934, the only elected government in Newfoundland was the St. John's municipal council.

From the very beginning, the relationship between the Carnell administration and Commission of Government was strained. The city refused a loan from the commission on the basis that it would mean control and interference in its affairs by that appointed body. Carnell made every effort to have the city's $1.5 million debt owed to government reduced, and his efforts proved somewhat successful. Carnell was a very popular mayor and was re-elected by acclamation in 1937. He signed an agreement during this term with Golden Arrow Coaches Limited to provide a bus service in parts of the city which didn't have the services of a streetcar. In the election of December 15, 1941, he was opposed by Picton R. MacCormac. Carnell was elected Mayor, and one of the first acts of his council was to appoint a commission of inquiry into the deplorable housing conditions in St. John's.

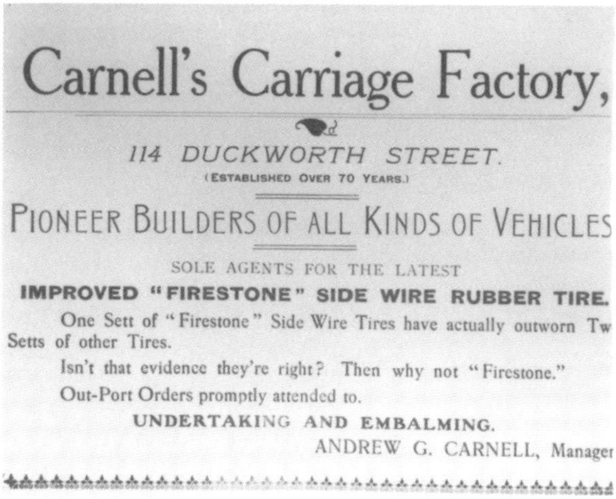

Advertisement for Carnell's Carriage factory and funeral home in 1906. (B.I.S. Centenary Book)

A thirteen-member commission of inquiry on housing and town planning was appointed on May 12, 1942 under the chairmanship of Supreme Court Justice Brian Dunfield. This commission submitted five reports and suggested the creation of a public housing corporation, separate and independent from the municipal council.

A tree-planting ceremony for a war memorial in 1939. King George V, Queen Elizabeth, Mayor Andrew G. Carnell. (Courtesy of Geoff Carnell, Jr.)

Mayor Andrew G. Carnell and Mayor LaGuardia in New York. (Photo by George Valiquette, News Consumer Ottawa. Courtesy of Geoffrey Carnell, Jr.

Among the highlights of Carnell's third term as Mayor (1941-1945) were reduction and adjustment in the city's funded debt and authorization for St. John's to issue bonds on the city's credit for an amount not beyond $3,000,000. He was instrumental in having the city's boundaries extended and enlarged the Bowring Park Committee to include three nominees from the Board of Trade, one of which had to be a member or representative of Bowring Brothers Limited.

Andrew G. Carnell speaking at the CLB Armoury. (Photo by Marshall Studios Ltd. Courtesy of Geoffrey Carnell, Jr.)

Carnell had built a strong populist support and in the November 13, 1945 election defeated contenders Eric Cook and James Gibbs, and he was again re-elected as Mayor. He established a number of committees during his term of office, including a six-man Traffic Control Committee. The sports-minded Carnell also had a committee established to study the feasibility of providing a new artificial ice rink for St. John's. The streetcar tracks were taken up, and the once familiar means of conveyance ceased operating on September 5, 1948. Carnell decided to try for an unprecented fifth term as Mayor in the election of November 8, 1949 and was defeated by Harry Mews. Andy Carnell died on January 26, 1951.

Henry G. R. Mews and the Confederation Era

Harry Mews was born in St. John's on December 18, 1897 and served in the Royal Newfoundland Regiment. After the First World War, he worked in Ontario until 1927. Then he returned to Newfoundland to work in the life insurance field. He became leader of the Progressive Conservatives who espoused the anti-Confederate cause and in the May 27, 1949 provincial general election, the first under Confederation with Canada, was a running mate with Michael Harrington in St. John's West. They were defeated by Liberals James Spratt and Oliver Vardy.

Mews turned his attention to municipal politics and on November 8, 1949 was elected Mayor of St. John's, defeating the ever popular Andy Carnell. The Mews administration succeeded in setting up an amiable relationship with the Smallwood Liberals despite their former adversarial positions. It received an interest-free loan of $150,000 from the province in 1950, and in 1952 the legislation provided for a city comptroller and city planning officer. The province also took over the city's financial obligation in the St. John's Housing Corporation.

Mews continued to gain popularity as a good administrator and was re-elected as Mayor by acclamation in the November 10, 1953 election. From 1953 to 1957, Mews saw the completion and opening of the St. John's Memorial Stadium. He oversaw the improvement of the city's water system, connecting up Petty Harbour Long Pond and was instrumental in increasing the size of Bowring Park by acquiring adjoining land. He ran for re-election on November 12, 1957 and was re-elected by acclamation.

One of the highlights of his tenure was the purchase of the privately owned Capital Coach Lines and setting up the St. John's Transportation Commission with control over bus operators. His administration was committed to providing public housing for low-income families and expanding suburban housing for the more affluent, and to that end he was successful in developing a number of areas in the northeast.

Mews entered the November 14, 1961 election with his mind made up to serve one last term. He easily defeated two opponents, John King and Robert Murphy. Some of the highlights of his last term in office were the development of the northeast land assembly, public housing in Buckmaster's Field, and urban renewal on New Gower Street where the present City Hall and Convention Centre now stand.

The new City Hall, built at a cost in 1970 of $3.5 million, was largely financed by a "secret fund" that Mews managed to accumulate over a period of nearly twenty years. He saw thc opening of a new swimming pool and facilities at Victoria Park on August 3, 1963 to replace the old familiar Tooton swimming pool, which served the West End so well over the years.

Mayor Henry G. R. Mews and Mayor William G. Adams laying the cornerstone of the new City Hall in 1969. (Courtesy of City Hall)

The Waterford Valley trunk sewer connecting St. John's with Mount Pearl was completed, and the old sanitary fill dump on Stamp's Lane was relocated to the present Robin Hood Bay site off Logy Bay Road.

This term ended Harry Mews's long involvement in municipal politics, for he did not seek office in the 1965 election. Upon his retirement from municipal politics, he devoted his leisure time to his various hobbies and business interests until his death on January 6, 1982.

William Adams
1965-1973
(Archives of St. John's City Hall)

Dorothy Wyatt
1973-1981
(Archives of St. John's City Hall)

Mayors of St. John's
1965-1997

John Murphy
1981-1990, 1993-1997
(Archives of St. John's City Hall)

Shannie Duff
1990-1993
(Archives of St. John's City Hall)

Councillors Added

The November 16, 1965 municipal election was contested by William G. Adams and Alec G. Henley for the position of Mayor, with the age qualification of householders being lowered from twenty-one to nineteen. Adams was elected. A lawyer, the new mayor was born in St. John's on June 17, 1923 and entered municipal politics in 1961. He served as Deputy Mayor from 1962 to 1965. Adams also entered provincial politics under the Smallwood administration and was elected Liberal Member for St. John's West in November, 1962.

The accomplishments of his first term included upgrading the city's water supply at Windsor Lake and an agreement with the provincial government to share half the cost of street paving. He opened a new municipal depot on Blackler Avenue and completed the Mundy Pond trunk sewer system.

Adams opened the recreation centre at Buckmaster's Field and a number of public housing units in the same area. During his first term, city council passed legislation entitling wives and husbands who were nineteen years of age and paying municipal taxes to vote. The same Act made provision to increase the number of councillors from six to eight. Adams sought re-election in the November 18, 1969 municipal election and defeated his only opponent, Alec G. Henley.

Mayor Adams's second term saw the completion of highway and arterial networks, neighbourhood improvement grants, and urban renewal in the Mundy Pond area. His administration also brought about changes in voting regulations whereby the vote was given to any Canadian citizen or British subject who was at least nineteen years old and a resident of the city for at least one year prior to a municipal election. In the ensuing election, he was defeated by the flamboyant Dorothy Wyatt.

First Woman Mayor

The November 13, 1973 municipal election was very colourful, as the incumbent Adams was challenged by the head-banded Mrs. Wyatt, who campaigned on the catchy slogan "Dorothy Wyatt won't be quiet." The mother of two, a registered nurse, defeated incumbent William Adams and contender Dr.

Patrick McNicholas and became the first woman elected to that position in the history of the city.

L-R: Councillor Brian Higgins; Mayor William Adams; City Clerk Edward Foran; Councillor Clarence Englebrecht (Bob Lewis); Councillor Al Andrews; Councillor Dorothy Wyatt being sworn in. November 18, 1969. (St. John's City Archives)

Born in St. John's, she held B.A. and B.Ed. degrees along with her Bachelor of Nursing and had a wide and varied career in business and nursing. During her first term of office, council approved a proposal for a major development on vacant land west of City Hall with Trizec Corporation of Montreal. The city later obtained control of the land when Trizec did not implement its plans. The oftentimes controversial municipal parking garage adjacent to Atlantic Place was completed during her term. Her administration had legislation enacted, granting the general public access to all public and special minutes of council for historic and academic reasons before 1925. One of the highlights of her first term in office was the hosting of the Canada Summer Games in St. John's in 1977.

The electorate were pleased with Mayor Wyatt's openness and accessibility during the first term in office and in the November 8, 1977 gave her a vote of confidence in electing her over Deputy Mayor John J. Murphy. Some of the highlights of Wyatt's second term as Mayor were the holding of the St. John's Day Celebration on June 24, 1978, approval and construction of the Toronto Dominion Building on Duckworth Street, and the implementation of a partial ward system for four areas of the city. She saw the completion of Pitts Memorial Drive (Harbour Arterial) in 1979 and the beginning of construction of Columbus Drive (Crosstown Arterial), opened in 1982.

Wyatt's administration had the city's taxation system changed from rental value to a capital-value base and approved a public housing project adjacent to Quidi Vidi Lake. Her bid for a third term having failed, she returned to private life as a nurse but re-emerged in the November 12, 1985 election and was elected councillor at large, a position she held until her death on September 23, 2001.

Dorothy Wyatt

Blending the Old and the New

The election of November 3, 1981 saw the re-emergence of businessman and former broadcaster John J. Murphy, who successfully contested the mayor's seat against incumbent Dorothy Wyatt and Councillor Ray O'Neill. Murphy was born in St. John's on September 24, 1922. He had served in such organizations as the St. John's Rotary Club (president), Newfoundland Board of Trade, and Junior Chamber of Commerce. He also had made a brief foray into provincial politics when he unsuccessfully contested St. John's East Extern as a Liberal candidate on September 8, 1966. He had served as a member of the Board of Regents of Memorial University and was a member of the Royal Commission on Education and Youth which reported in 1967.

John Murphy's experience as the sole commissioner for Plan 91 pertaining to a plan for the city for the last quarter of the century gained him respect and confidence. He had a genuine concern for low- and middle-income housing and improved recreational facilities, which earned him a second term as Mayor when he was elected by acclamation on November 12, 1985. During his term as Mayor, St. John's almost doubled in geographic size with the acquisition of Kilbride, Shea Heights, Airport Heights, and Freshwater Bay. He concentrated his efforts in building up the inner core of old St. John's with the erection of infill housing and was instrumental in introducing the Neighbourhood Improvement and Residential Rehabilitation Programs, which provided low-interest loans and grants to improve approximately 3,000 homes while keeping their unique and distinctive architectural character. His efforts in providing an inspection service saw the use of fireproof materials and elimination of disaster-ridden oil burners in many older homes.

Mayor Murphy directed the expansion of Prince Philip Drive, Kenmount and Logy Bay Roads during his term in office. He has also seen the introduction of cable television to the council chamber. Some of the other highlights of his term as Mayor were hosting His Holiness Pope John Paul II, The Prince of Wales, and Princess Diana. He was very much involved in the 400th anniversary of the founding of the British Empire in North America by Sir Humphrey Gilbert, which was celebrated in 1983.

Murphy was succeeded by Mrs. Shannie Duff in the municipal election of November 13, 1990. He returned to public life in November 9, 1993 when he was elected Mayor for a third time. One of the many highlights of his term was the Cabot Celebrations associated with the 500th anniversary of the discovery of Newfoundland by the Italian explorer John Cabot. He unsuccessfully contested his fourth and fifth attempts to become Mayor on September 30, 1997 and September 25, 2001 when he lost to populist Andy Wells both times.

Mayor Suzanne Duff and Environmental Issues

November 13, 1990 saw the election of the second woman to hold the position of Mayor of St. John's. Shannie Duff was born in St. John's on July 22, 1936 and was founding president of Avalon Cablevision Ltd. in 1975. She was elected to the St. John's City Council in 1977 and Progressive Conservative Member of the House of Assembly for St. John's East in 1989. Mrs. Duff was actively involved in a number of organizations such as the St. John's Heritage Foundation and the Newfoundland Historic Trust in the 1970s. In the 1981 municipal election, she polled the highest number of votes in that election and thereby became Deputy Mayor.

St. John's first mayor George Shea and council, 1902. The St. John's municipal council was first established in 1888, but it was not until 1902 that legislation was passed to permit the election of a mayor and six councillors. (St. John's City Archives)

St. John's City Council 1997-2001
(Courtesy of Bob Crocker)

Front Row (L-R): Councillor Dorothy Wyatt; Councillor Dennis O'Keefe; Mayor Andrew Wells; Councillor John Dinn; Deputy Mayor Marie White.

Back Row (L-R): Councillor Peter Miller; Councillor Suzanne Duff; Councillor Keith Coombs; Councillor Gerry Colbert; Councillor Frank Galgay; Councillor Sean Hanrahan.

During her term as Mayor, Mrs. Duff demonstrated a strong commitment to protecting the environment and dealing with environmental issues. She was instrumental in hiring an Environmental Initiatives Manager, appointing an Environmental Advisory Committee. One of her concerns was the need of reviewing all Development Regulations to ensure that they adhered to the overall concept of sustainable development. Through her efforts, a new community agency, the St. John's Clean and Beautiful, was established with a mandate to involve all citizens in efforts to reduce litter, improve waste handling, and beautify the city.

Mrs. Duff was a strong advocate in advancing activities associated with enhancing the environment. Her leadership was evident in undertaking a major study of the wetlands and waterways and providing support for various community groups working to protect and enhance the city rivers. She saw the establishment of the Atlantic Coastal Action Program, whose mandate was to assess the problem of pollution in St. John's Harbour and recommend ways and means to rectify the problem. Mrs. Duff continued her commitment to the environment in supporting and encouraging community environmental activities such as leaf composting, Christmas tree recycling, and tree planting. The establishment of environmental industries for metal shredding, recycling, and handling of septic and hazardous waste was also encouraged.

Mrs. Duff had a strong commitment to improved housing, beginning with her first election to city council in 1977. When she was Deputy Mayor from 1981 to 1990, she chaired the city's housing committee, resulting in the city's award-winning non-profit housing program.

During her term as Mayor, the geographic size of St. John's increased with the acquisition of Wedgewood Park and the Goulds and added new responsibilities such as the Regional Water and Fire Services and the Aquarena. The accumulated deficit had reached approximately $4.9 million by 1991, and she committed to put the city on a sound financial footing before she left office. However, she was defeated in the November 9, 1993 municipal election by John J. Murphy.

Mayor Andrew Wells and the New Millennium

The outspoken, controversial and hard-working Andy Wells, born in Corner Brook on August 26, 1944, was sworn in as Mayor of St. John's on October 31, 1997 after defeating businessman and politician Walter Carter, former provincial Cabinet Minister Jerry Dinn, and lawyer, member of the House of Assembly, and Leader of the New Democratic Party of Newfoundland and Labrador, Jack Harris. Mr. Wells brought with his position twenty years' experience on city council, providing him an excellent opportunity of acquiring insight into the political and business life of the province and the complexities of intergovernmental relations. A drawn-out recount requested by Jack Harris delayed Mr. Wells's swearing in until October 31, 1997.

Mayor Andrew Wells
1997-2005
(Archives of St. John's City Hall)

Mr. Wells is a graduate of Prince of Wales Collegiate and Memorial University of Newfoundland. He served as a member of the Royal Commission on Employment and Unemployment and a member of the Board of Commissioners of Public Utilities. He has had considerable experience in labour and industrial relations, having served as Business Agent with the Newfoundland and Labrador Nurses' Union, National Representative with the Canadian Union of Public Employees, President of the Newfoundland and Labrador Division, Canadian Union of Public Employees, General Vice-President of Canadian Union of Public Employees, Regional Vice-President, Canadian Union of Public Employees. During his career, he was a production assistant and producer-director with the Education Television Centre of Memorial University and had a brief radio career as host of CJYQ's *Straight Talk*.

Mayor Wells was a strong proponent of Southlands becoming part of St. John's rather than Mount Pearl. The provincial government appointed former Lieutenant-Governor Frederick Russell as Commissioner, and after a number of public hearings he recommended that Southlands remain with the City of St. John's. The provincial government accepted his recommendation.

The St. John's Harbour cleanup has always been a source of concern for the previous city councils. During the present term of Mayor Andy Wells, the City of St. John's and Department of National Defence signed a letter whereby the city was given access to land on the Southside for purposes of constructing a pump-house. This significant milestone initiated the beginning of the Harbour Cleanup Project, which will be implemented in a number of phases over the next twenty years. This will be a cost-shared project among the federal, provincial and municipal governments within the region, at a cost of approximately $150 million.

Mayor Wells has always been an advocate of the amalgamation of Mount Pearl with St. John's and is a strong proponent of Donovans Industrial Park becoming part of the city of St. John's. This issue continues to be an ongoing debate. During the early days of Mayor Wells's term of office, the city assumed control of the Civic Centre Corporation and has proceeded with a site selection and the pre-qualification of architects/project managers for the Civic Centre/Convention Centre Complex. It was first announced that the project would cost approximately $36 million to be jointly funded by the federal, provincial and municipal levels of government. The Mile One Civic Centre opened in May, 2001.

Among the other issues addressed during Mayor Wells's early term of office have been the expenditure of funds to conduct a study into the feasibility of widening the Narrows to accommodate cruise ships. This project has been completed and will be a very important contributing factor to the increase of tourism in the city, according to Mayor Wells. Upon the initiative of the mayor, the city of St. John's accepted the report of Cabot Martin respecting the issues relating to the relocation of engineering and procurement staff by the Terra Nova Consortium from England to St. John's.

In 1998, the city commenced an action in the Supreme Court of Newfoundland against the Canada-Newfoundland Offshore Petroleum Board and the Proponents of the Terra Nova Oil and Gas Field Development in an attempt to compel the Board to enforce the following conditions:

As soon as possible after Project Sanction, the proponent relocate engineering and procurement activities for the Project to Newfoundland.

Following discussions with the Proponent, the Board accepted that for cost and scheduling reasons it was not practical to move the engineering activities to Newfoundland.

The court agreed with the position of the city that the condition had not been met but decided that the Board did not have a statutory duty to enforce their order and could not be forced to do so. The court also decided that the city did not have the legal capacity or status to take the action.

On July 27, 2000, the Government of Newfoundland and Labrador announced its decision to relocate 278 civil service positions outside St. John's in various rural areas of the province under a regionalization initiative. Mayor Wells condemned the relocation plan because of the undue hardship caused to the lives of those individuals being relocated. His opposition to the decision, in addition to the personal hardships, was the cost, estimated by the Newfoundland Association of Public Employees to be between $23 million and $26 million, compared to a government estimate of $7 million. He suggested that the government establish a long-term plan for reorganization with decentralization of services based on legitimate criteria and any monies saved by the postponement of the relocation plan be placed in a rural development fund to provide economic development in rural areas of the province.

Mayor Andy Wells led the city of St. John's into the new millennium. His term of office has proven very challenging and exciting as the city faced unprecedented growth and progress. He was elected for a second term as Mayor of St. John's on September 25, 2001.

Appendices

PRESENT-DAY ST. JOHN'S CITY HALL. (ST. JOHN'S CITY ARCHIVES)

Appendix A

City Council Members 1888-1997

August 30, 1888

MUNICIPAL ELECTION

Ward 1 John T. Carnell
Ward 2 Francis St. John
Ward 3 Moses Monroe
Ward 4 Michael Power
Ward 5 William Morison

Government appointees on council: James Goodfellow, chairman and James P. Fox. The Hon. J. Harris succeeded James P. Fox, who died before the end of his term.

This was the first municipal election in St. John's and the first election under the Ballot Act.

January 23, 1892

Second MUNICIPAL ELECTION

Ward 1 John T. Carnell
Ward 2 John T. Southcott
Ward 3 James Goodfellow
Ward 4 Michael Power
Ward 5 Donald Morison

Appointees to council: Edward W. Bennett and Thomas Mitchell. On February 26, 1892, Mitchell was elected chairman. In 1894, James J. Callahan was appointed to council.

1893

By-election, John Harris elected following the death of John Carnell.

1893

T. G. Chapman of Plymouth, England was to be engaged as City Engineer. See Minute of April 8, 1893, page 105.

December 30, 1893

Chairman Thomas Mitchell was replaced by Thomas J. Edens.

January 4, 1894

Councillor Power was elected chairman.

1894

John Harris was elected in a by-election following the death of Carnell in 1893.

January 23, 1896

MUNICIPAL ELECTION

Ward 1 John Harris
Ward 2 Thomas Keating
Ward 3 John V. O'Dea
Ward 4 Michael Power
Ward 5 James T. Callahan

Appointments by government: Thomas J. Edens and R. A. McCoubrey.

The new council held its first meeting on February 7, 1896 and Power was elected chairman.

1898 - 1902

St. John's was governed by commission. Three members were appointed by government consisting of: H. C. Burchell, T. M. White and J. V. O'Dea.

1899

P. C. O'Driscoll succeeded T. M. White who resigned.

1900

O'Driscoll and O'Dea resigned and H. F. Bradshaw was appointed.

1902

Abolishment of the commission.

1902

Legislation was passed providing for an elected council consisting of a mayor and six councillors, all elected at large. Elections were to be held in June of every fourth year from 1902 onwards.

June 19, 1902

MUNICIPAL ELECTION

Mayor:
George Shea

Councillors:
John R. Bennett
William J. Ellis
Charles F. Muir
John Harris
John Anderson
Michael Kennedy

Bennett received the highest vote among the six and was referred to as Senior Councillor and as such was to preside over council meetings in the absence of the mayor.

June 26, 1906

MUNICIPAL ELECTION

Mayor:
Michael P. Gibbs

Councillors:
William J. Ellis
Michael Kennedy
John Carew
Samuel G. Collier
John Cowan
James T. Martin

In September 1906 John Carew died in office, no by-election was held.

July 1908

First civic strike—sanitary workers.

June 27, 1910

MUNICIPAL ELECTION

Mayor:
William J. Ellis

Councillors:
James Martin
John Coaker
James J. Channing
Charles R. Ryan
James J. Mullaly
Martin W. Myrick

August 9, 1911

Council opened the town's first civic-owned offices after having purchased the Seaman's Home in late 1910.

July 1, 1914

Elected form of municipal government replaced by commission system of government.

Appointments:
John Anderson
Charles P. Ayre
F. W. Bradshaw
William J. Ellis
William G. Gosling
John Harris
Edward M. Jackman
James McGrath
Francis MacNamara
Isaac C. Morris
James J. Mullaly
J. W. Withers

July 2, 1914

First meeting of commission. Gosling elected as chairman, defeating Ellis. Ellis resigned after failing to become chairman.

June 29, 1916

MUNICIPAL ELECTION

Mayor:
William G. Gosling

Councillors:
Isaac C. Morris
Dr. James S. Tait
Henry J. Brownrigg
James J. Mullaly
Charles P. Ayre
Nicholas J. Vinnicombe

June 1920 - June 1921

St. John's run by commission appointed by the Governor-in-Council.

July 5, 1920

Appointments:
William G. Gosling
Charles P. Ayre
Isaac C. Morris
James Mullaly
Nicholas J. Vinnicombe

August 2, 1921

Civic legislation known as the City Charter passed both Houses of the Legislature. This document was worked on extensively by William G. Gosling and laid out the rights and responsibilities of the council and its officials. Women received the right to vote as a result of the charter.

July 1 - December 31, 1921

New commission appointed to replace the one that went out of office June 30, 1921.

June 26, 1921

New commission took office.

Appointments:
Isaac C. Morris, Chairman
Samuel G. Collier
W. H. Jackman
James J. Mullaly
Samuel H. Peet
Nicholas J. Vinnicombe

The old commission ended its term of office on June 30, 1921 and the new commission took office on July 26, 1921, leaving St. John's without any local government for nearly a month.

December 15, 1921
MUNICIPAL ELECTION

Mayor:
Tasker Cook

Councillors:
James T. Martin
Philip E. Outerbridge
Nicholas J. Vinnicombe
Samuel G. Collier
Charles W. Ryan
Reginald Dowden

The new position of Deputy Mayor was to be determined by a vote of all the council.

December 8, 1925
MUNICIPAL ELECTION

Mayor:
Tasker Cook

Councillors:
Joseph Fitzgibbon
Dr. Archibald C. Tait
William E. Brophy
Philip E. Outerbridge
Charles W. Ryan
James T. Martin

Julia Salter Earle ran in this election and came within eleven votes of claiming the sixth and final council seat. This was the first election in which women were allowed to run for council. Three women ran unsuccessfully.

1927

City's first Town Planning Commission appointed.

December 9, 1929

MUNICIPAL ELECTION

Mayor:
Charles J. Howlett

Councillors:
Charles W. Ryan
Andrew G. Carnell
John P. Kelly
Jonas C. Barter
James R. Chalker
Ernest St. Clair Churchill

Carnell was elected Deputy Mayor.

March 31, 1932

Charles J. Howlett died. Carnell administered the city.

1933

MUNICIPAL ELECTION

Mayor:
Andrew G. Carnell

Councillors:
James R. Chalker
Charles W. Ryan

John P. Kelly
Philip E. Outerbridge
Michael F. Caul
James J. Spratt

Chalker elected as Deputy Mayor. Outerbridge resigns shortly afterwards.

April 8, 1935

By-election

John Williams wins seat left vacant by Outerbridge.

1937

MUNICIPAL ELECTION

Mayor:
Andrew G. Carnell

Councillors:
James R. Chalker
James J. Spratt
John P. Kelly
John M. Tobin
Kenneth Ruby
John T. Meaney

Chalker elected as Deputy Mayor.

December 15, 1941

MUNICIPAL ELECTION

Mayor:
Andrew G. Carnell

Councillors:
Eric Cook

Edward Lawrence
Oliver L. Vardy
James J. Spratt
John P. Kelly
John T. Meaney

1943

Lawrence and Meaney died while in office. Their seats were filled by A. M. Fraser and Henry G. R. Mews in a by-election later that same year.

November 13, 1945

MUNICIPAL ELECTION

Mayor:
Andrew G. Carnell

Councillors:
James J. Spratt
Henry G. R. Mews
Oliver L. Vardy
John P. Kelly
William P. Ryan
Eric Jerrett

Spratt was chosen as Deputy Mayor by council. A tradition had evolved whereby the deputy mayor's position was given to the councillor finishing first in the polls.

November 8, 1949

MUNICIPAL ELECTION

Mayor:
Henry G. R. Mews

Deputy Mayor:
George Nightingale

Councillors:
James D. Higgins
Joseph Fitzgibbon
Eric Jerrett
James R. W. Tucker
Leo A. Earle

February 1950

Eric Jerrett died and was replaced on council by Douglas Oliphant who won the by-election that same year.

November 10, 1953

MUNICIPAL ELECTION

Mayor:
Henry G. R. Mews

Deputy Mayor:
James D. Higgins

Councillors:
George Nightingale
Joseph Fitzgibbon
James R. W. Tucker
Leo A. Earle
W. Gordon Warren

November 12, 1957

MUNICIPAL ELECTION

Mayor:
Henry G. R. Mews

Deputy Mayor:
James D. Higgins

Councillors:
Joseph Fitzgibbon
James R. W. Tucker
George Nightingale
Geoffrey C. Carnell
Alec G. Henley

March 31, 1958

Tucker resigned, succeeded by Robert F. MacLeod who won a by-election later that year.

November 14, 1961

MUNICIPAL ELECTION

Mayor:
Henry G. R. Mews

Deputy Mayor:
William G. Adams

Councillors:
James D. Higgins
Geoffrey C. Carnell
Alec G. Henley
Walter C. Carter
James M. Fagan

September 1963

Higgins resigned.

November 1963

By-election

Gerald A. Wiggins elected.

November 1964

Wiggins died.

December 1965
MUNICIPAL ELECTION

Mayor:
William G. Adams

Deputy Mayor:
John Crosbie

Councillors:
Walter C. Carter
James Fagan
Geoffrey C. Carnell
Thomas Doyle
Jim Browne

July 1966
Crosbie resigned from council.

November 15, 1966
By-election

Clarence L. Englebrecht (Bob Lewis) was elected.

1968
Carter resigned from council.

November 18, 1969
MUNICIPAL ELECTION

Mayor:
William G. Adams

Deputy Mayor:
Leonard Stirling

Councillors:
Clarence Englebrecht (Bob Lewis)
James Fagan
Brian E. Higgins
Dorothy Wyatt
Jim Browne
Albert Andrews
Geoffrey C. Carnell

Wyatt was the first woman ever elected to council.

November 13, 1973

MUNICIPAL ELECTION

Mayor:
Dorothy Wyatt

Deputy Mayor:
John J. Murphy

Councillors:
Miller Ayre
David G. Riche
David Barrett
James Fagan
Brian E. Higgins
Eric Gullage
Raymond A. O'Neill

Wyatt became St. John's first female mayor.

October 26, 1976

Eric Gullage resigned.

December 1976

Ted Henley was appointed as first City Manager.

November 8, 1977
MUNICIPAL ELECTION

Mayor:
Dorothy Wyatt

Deputy Mayor:
Raymond A. O'Neill

Councillors:
Suzanne Duff
Brian E. Higgins
James Fagan
David Barrett
Frances Innis
Hugh Baird
Andrew Wells

Council took office on December 1, 1977. Previous councils had taken office on January 1 of the year following the election.

June 24, 1978
First St. John's Day celebrations.

April 1979
Brian Higgins died.

September 25, 1979
Thomas Osborne elected in a by-election.

November 3, 1981
MUNICIPAL ELECTION

Mayor:
John J. Murphy

Deputy Mayor:
Suzanne Duff

Councillors at large:
James Fagan
David Barrett
Ronald Pumphrey
Ward 1: Andrew Wells
Ward 2: John Tessier
Ward 3: Bruce Tilley
Ward 4: Thomas Osborne

December 1, 1981

Council took office.

September 1984

Ronald Pumphrey resigned.

November 12, 1985

MUNICIPAL ELECTION

Mayor:
John J. Murphy

Deputy Mayor:
Suzanne Duff

Councillors at large:
Raymond A. O'Neill
Dorothy Wyatt
David Barrett
Ward 1: Andrew Wells
Ward 2: Eric Gullage
Ward 3: Bruce Tilley
Ward 4: Thomas Osborne

May 24, 1989

Eric Gullage resigns.

November 13, 1990

MUNICIPAL ELECTION

Mayor:
Suzanne Duff

Deputy Mayor:
Andrew Wells

Councillors at large:
Dorothy Wyatt
Raymond A. O'Neill
Basil Jamieson
Ward 1: Wendy Williams
Ward 2: Douglas Atkinson
Ward 3: John Whalen
Ward 4: Gerard Colbert

February 25, 1992

By-election—Wards 5 and 6

Ward 5: Paul J. Reynolds
Ward 6: John Dinn

Wards 5 and 6 were added after the Towns of Wedgewood Park and the Goulds amalgamated with St. John's.

September 28, 1992

Councillor Atkinson resigns.

November 24, 1992
By-election Ward 2.

Bruce Tilley elected.

December 7, 1992
Bruce Tilley sworn in.

February 1993
William K. Mann hired as City Manager.

November 9, 1993
MUNICIPAL ELECTION

Mayor:
John J. Murphy

Deputy Mayor:
Andrew Wells

Councillors at large:
Dorothy Wyatt
Jeffrey Brace
Marie White
Raymond A. O'Neill
Ward 1: Sean Hanrahan
Ward 2: Shawn Skinner
Ward 3: Keith Coombs
Ward 4: Gerry Colbert
Ward 5: John Dinn

September 30, 1997
MUNICIPAL ELECTION

Mayor:
Andrew Wells

Deputy Mayor:
Marie White

Councillors at large:
Peter Miller
Suzanne Duff
Dennis O'Keefe
Dorothy Wyatt
Ward 1: Sean Hanrahan
Ward 2: Frank Galgay
Ward 3: Keith Coombs
Ward 4: Gerry Colbert
Ward 5: John Dinn

October 14, 1997
Council sworn in. Deputy Mayor Marie White sworn in as Acting Mayor due to a recount of the mayor's vote.

October 31, 1997
Andrew Wells sworn in as Mayor.

September 25, 2001
MUNICIPAL ELECTION

Mayor:
Andrew Wells

Deputy Mayor:
Gerry Colbert

Councillors at large:
Dennis O'Keefe
Shannie Duff
Paul Sears
Dorothy Wyatt
Ward 1: Arthur Puddister
Ward 2: Frank Galgay
Ward 3: Keith Coombs
Ward 4: Kevin Breen
Ward 5: John Dinn

October 9, 2001

Council sworn in. Councillor Dorothy Wyatt passed away on September 23, 2001. She was the first person ever to be elected posthumously to St. John's City Council.

December 3, 2001

Councillor at large Sandy Hickman sworn in to replace Councillor Dorothy Wyatt who passed away on September 23, 2001.

Appendix B

Partial List of Shipwrecks Near St. John's

Agenria: Brig lost off Cape Spear, 1834.

Athlon: Schooner lost at Blackhead February 1, 1918.

Avalon: Brigantine belonging to William Walsh lost under South Head, Narrows, February 1, 1848. Five men, Michael Halley, Patrick Condon, James Kelly, John McDonald and Patrick Walsh, 18-year-old son of the owner were drowned.

HMS *Avenger*: sixteen-gun sloop of war lost off St. John's October 8, 1912.

Bullbird: Schooner lost in the Narrows May 2, 1925.

Canada: Canadian Vessel lost on Pancake Shoal December 16, 1811.

Dorothy Melita: Schooner sank near Cape Spear March 28, 1935.

SS *Earl*: Sealing vessel lost off St. John's July 23, 1850.

SS *Edmund Donald*: Vessel towed out of St. John's and burned November 19, 1932.

Ellen: Schooner lost in the Narrows December 26, 1818. Six men drowned.

Elsie: Schooner sunk after colliding with the schooner *Northern Light* which also sank off South Head November 7, 1884. Two men drowned in the accident.

Emblem: Schooner sunk in collision off Sugar Loaf March 29, 1929.

Fane: Schooner lost at Cuckold's Cove August 17, 1817.

Favourable: Schooner caught fire and burned in St. John's Harbour December 2, 1901.

Geisha: Schooner lost in ice off Cape Spear June 6, 1909.

Grand Master: Small schooner lost off St. John's May 23, 1896.

Hannah: Schooner lost at Cuckhold's Cove October 19, 1933.

Helen: Schooner lost in the Narrows May 2, 1925.

Ich Dien: Lunenburg schooner caught fire and burned in St. John's Harbour October 20, 1909.

Ida: Brig lost in the Narrows January 2, 1876.

*Juli*a: 144-ton brigantine lost in the Narrows October 17, 1876. The vessel was owned by G. J. Hayward & Company. She cleared for the Mediterranean with 3,000 quintals of fish as cargo.

Luetta: Schooner lost in the Narrows September 19, 1921.

Maggie: Schooner cut down in the Narrows November 7, 1896. Fourteen people drowned.

Magnolia: Schooner wrecked in Freshwater Bay December 24, 1872.

Marcella: Brig burned in St. John's Harbour July 14, 1846.

Marguerite: A Spanish vessel capsized at L. O'Brien's wharf September 6, 1861.

SS *Marsland*: 4,000-ton steamer went aground on Vestal Rock in the Narrows July 2, 1933, became total wreck.

Mary Pittman: Schooner lost on Chain Rock November 21, 1856.

Mary Ann: Schooner from Northern Bay sunk in collision with the schooner *Somerset* near Sugar Loaf September 24, 1886. Four men drowned.

Mazaguenzama: Spanish brigantine lost near Blackhead August 14, 1876. Captain Fiol, wife and child drowned. St. John's Harbour at the time was filled with smoke from a fire on the Southside Hills.

Notting Hill: Vessel sank off St. John's February 11, 1884.

Paradise: Western boat from Placentia Bay lost North Head, in the Narrows December 4, 1811.

Pink: English schooner from Hamburg with general cargo lost in the Narrows October 2, 1866.

Phoebe: Schooner lost in Narrows November 13, 1909.

Phoco: Schooner sank in the Narrows March 2, 1870. One man named Ryan drowned.

Rosalin: Schooner sank off St. John's May 2, 1872.

Salmah: Schooner lost at Cape Spear November 17, 1866. Three crew members drowned, remainder saved by James Cantwell and his sons.

Sea Skipper: Vessel lost off Sugar Loaf July 19, 1812.

Shamrock: Vessel lost in the Narrows November 17, 1902.

Stella: Schooner wrecked at Cuckhold's Cove June 17, 1904.

Souris Bell: Schooner cut down in the Narrows June 2, 1909 by steamship. Great loss of life.

Tulip: Schooner lost in the Narrows October 10, 1921.

Vernie May: Schooner lost off Sugar Loaf May 28, 1929.

Vulture: Channel Islands schooner lost in the Narrows August 2, 1812. Hull later salvaged and repaired.

Wild Briar: Schooner wrecked in Freshwater Bay October 5, 1934. Crew were rescued.

Appendix C

Interesting Events in St. John's History

January 2, 1886

First Salvation Army service in Newfoundland held, in Victoria Hall, one man and three girls present.

January 3, 1837

Newfoundland British Society established January 3, 1837.

January 5, 1917

Harvey & Company presented three and one half acres of land to City of St. John's for workingmen's homes.

January 6, 1850

First Mass celebrated in the Roman Catholic Cathedral, now Basilica, by Bishop Fleming.

January 9, 1936

Gosling Library first opened.

January 10, 1848

A night patrol first established in St. John's, consisting of sixteen specials and four constables under the management of High Constable Finlay.

January 21, 1870

Avalon Skating Rink opened by Governor Hill.

January 25, 1942

Trial blackout at midnight in St. John's.

January 30, 1876

Irish Christian Brothers opened their first school in St. John's in the Benevolent Irish Society's Hall.

February 2, 1859

Smith O'Brien, Irish patriot, arrived in St. John's in a Cunard steamer, which was short of coal and was accorded an ovation by the citizens.

February 3, 1834

Mrs. Mary Traverse refused to give up the furniture of the House of Assembly which she had attached until her rent for the Assembly rooms had been paid.

February 5, 1806

First meeting to consider the founding of the Benevolent Irish Society held at the London Tavern.

February 7, 1864

First stone for St. Patrick's Church, Riverhead, hauled by Cathedral Fire Brigade.

February 11, 1890

St. John's City Council decided to import steamroller for use on city streets.

February 14, 1823

St. John's first public library established, afterwards called the Athenaeum.

February 15, 1852

House of Assembly voted 100 pounds for night police to do duty in the city.

February 28, 1871

St. John's Star of the Sea Society formally instituted in the Fishermen's Hall.

March 1, 1884

Metropolitan Club formed in St. John's. C. J. Harvey, chairman; T. J. Murphy, treasurer; James Milley, secretary.

March 6, 1847

Ninety-five vessels cleared for the seal-fishery from St. John's.

March 9, 1880

St. Thomas's and St. Mary's Temperance Societies formed.

March 10, 1875

Riot at Fox's wharf; crews of the sealing steamers *Greenland* and *Iceland* attacked St. John's men, and a general melee ensued. Considerable damage done to both steamers.

March 13, 1833

Notice first given in House of Assembly for bill to incorporate St. John's, by Newman W. Hoyles.

March 15, 1881

Citizens of all denominations began hauling stone for Church of England Cathedral.

March 16, 1878

Headstones smashed in Riverhead cemetery.

March 20, 1878

First telephone in Newfoundland set up in St. John's, linking the houses of John Delaney and John Higgins.

March 24, 1846

St. John's, Newfoundland Auxiliary Bible Society founded. Honourable William Thomas, president.

March 25, 1893

Agnes Cowan, Matron of St. John's Hospital, died.

March 29, 1864

First duty put on coal in St. John's (twenty cents per ton).

April 1, 1854

Steer & Ayre opened business.

April 5, 1894

First lodge (Far East) Knights of Pythias formed in St. John's.

April 14, 1711

Captain Hayden was the Fishing Admiral of St. John's Harbour and Captain Dorrel was Vice-Admiral.

April 15, 1863

First ladies employed in a dry goods store in St. John's.

April 21, 1898

Michael Cullen remained in a hypnotic sleep in the Total Abstinence Hall window for twenty-four hours, under the influence of Professor Lawrence.

April 23, 1880

Baird Brothers' windows broken, presumed by members or friends of the Early Closing Association, because this firm first broke the rules for closing. The clerks met and repudiated the conduct.

April 29, 1876

Don Carlos, Spanish Pretender, arrived in St. John's in SS *Hibernia*, en route to Baltimore. He travelled under the name Edwardo Gonzalos.

May 7, 1864

Trees in Soldier Meadow (near Railway Station) planted.

May 13, 1861

Election riots in St. John's. Soldiers fired and Thomas Clifford and William Fitzptrick were killed. Fr. O'Donel, Patrick Myrick, and others were wounded. On this same date in 1954 the first television was seen in St. John's. It was a freak reception from New Jersey.

May 17, 1857

Arch and statue of St. John the Baptist erected in front of Roman Catholic Cathedral (Basilica) grounds.

May 19, 1876

Terra Nova Skating and Curling Club organized in St. John's.

May 25, 1849

General Protestant Cemetery, Riverhead, first opened.

May 26, 1849

First velocipede rode in public. R. H. Earles went beyond Topsail and returned.

May 27, 1827

Orphan Asylum first opened.

June 10, 1842

Arrival of first Mercy Sisters in St. John's.

June 14, 1871

The Carter Monument, Government House, unveiled.

June 16, 1862

First water to St. John's from Windsor Lake turned on.

June 22, 1897

Cornerstone of Cabot Tower laid by Bishop M. Howley.

June 24, 1820

Masonic Lodge No. 226 dined in St. John's at the Crown & Anchor tavern. Richard Holden, secretary.

June 25, 1849

Church of England Cemetery, Forest Road, consecrated.

July 1, 1855

Belvedere Cemetery consecrated by Bishop Mullock.

July 8, 1892

St. John's devastated by the greatest fire in its history.

July 15, 1935

Railway Employees Welfare Association erected thirty-eight houses in area between Craigmillar Avenue and Topsail Road.

July 23, 1890

Two earthquake shocks felt at blockhouse, St. John's.

August 14, 1842

Presbyterian Church first organized in St. John's.

August 22, 1888

Sir Ambrose Shea entertained Prince George (Duke of York) with a grand ball.

August 27, 1806

First St. John's newspaper, *Royal Gazette*, published. And Billy Barnes, the first newsboy, appeared on the streets of St. John's.

September 1, 1892

Evening Telegram restarted.

September 2, 1796

Fleet of French ships appeared off St. John's Harbour.

September 4, 1874

Lord Charles Beresford visited St. John's during delay of SS *Nova Scotia* en route to USA.

September 8, 1863

Sixty-two stowaways landed from SS *Adriatic*, a Galway steamer.

September 9, 1855

Roman Catholic Cathedral (Basilica) consecrated.

September 10, 1888

Great open-air meeting to protest against sending a confederation delegate to Canada.

September 18, 1895

J. H. Noonan of Her Majesty's Customs seized this day a case of claret, landed from the French ship *La Clochetere* and intended as a present for Judge Prowse. It was found in the Harbour Master's office. The Judge subsequently got his wine on paying the duty.

September 25, 1895

Fire Brigade absorbed in constabulary under Inspector-General McCowan.

September 28, 1836

St. Thomas's Anglican Church opened.

September 29, 1861

Prince Napoleon arrived in St. John's in his yacht *Jerome.*

October 8, 1899

The Twentieth Century Fund started in Cochrane Street Church.

October 13, 1876

Scottish Kirk (Free St. Andrew's) Duckworth Street burned.

October 14, 1850

First steam tug seen in St. John's, the *St. George*, arrived.

October 24, 1794

Lieutenant Lawry killed while leading a press gang in St. John's.

November 1, 1886

The streets of St. John's first lit by electricity.

November 5, 1840

Arrival of HMS *Spitfire,* first steamer ever to enter St. John's.

November 14, 1895

Superintendent Sullivan (police) suspended from position for refusing to remove A. B. Morine from courthouse at request of Judge Prowse.

November 20, 1899

Elder Webber, pastor of Adventist Church, died.

November 23, 1921

Rotary Club formed. Harry E. Cowan first president.

November 25, 1855

The following new streets were named in St. John's: Victoria, Cathedral, Darling, and Chapel.

December 3, 1843

St. Andrew's Presbyterian Kirk, Harvey Road, opened.

December 10, 1894

Crosbie Hotel opened.

December 12, 1901

Guglielmo Marconi received the first transatlantic wireless signal at Signal Hill.

December 14, 1711

J. Crowe, Commodore of the Newfoundland convoy, reported the total population residing permanently in Newfoundland, including men, women, children, and servants was about 2,281.

December 21, 1894

Bank of Nova Scotia began business in St. John's.

December 25, 1895

First Midnight Mass in Roman Catholic Cathedral (Basilica).

December 26, 1899

First Orange Society parade in St. John's.

December 31, 1817

Governor Pickmore offered 300 pounds reward for apprehension of person who tried to burn William Hogan's house in Maggoty Cove.

Appendix D

Letters from St. John's

John Rut's Letter of 1527

The first-known letter to have been written from St. John's was that of John Rut in 1527, just thirty years after Cabot's discovery of Newfoundland. The letter was written to King Henry VIII who had financed the Rut expedition to Newfoundland:

> Pleasing your Honourable Grace to heare of your servant John Rut with all his company here in good health thanks be to God and your Graceship- the Mary of Gilford with all her—— thanks be to God- and if it please your honourable Grace we ranne in our course to the Northward, till we camwe to 53 degrees, there we found many great islands of ice and deepe water; we found no soundings and then we durst not go further to the Northward for fear of more ice, and then we cast about to the Southward, and within foure days after we had one hundred and sixty fathoms and then we came into 52 degrees and fell in with the mayne land and within ten leagues of the mayne land we met with a great island of ice and came hard by her for it was standing in deep water and so went to Cape de Bas a good Harbour and many small islands and a great fresh river going up farre into the mayne land and the mayne land all wilderness and mountains and woodes and no natural ground but all mosse and no inhabitants nor no people in these parts; and in the woods we found footings of divers great beasts but we saw none not in ten leagues- and please your Grace the Sampson and wee kept company all the way till within two days before we met with all the Islands of ice; that was the first day of July at night and there arose a great and a marvellous great storme and much foul weather- I trust in the Almightie Jesu to heare good newes of her-and please your Grace we were considering and a

writing of all our order, how we would wash us, and what course we would draw when God doe send foul weather, that with the Cape de Sper shee should go - and he that come first should tarry the space of sixe weeks one for another, and watered at Cape de Bas ten days ordering of your Grace and fishing, and so departed to the Southward to seek our fellow; the third day of August we entered a good harbour we entered into a good harbour called St. John and thence found Eleuen Saile of Normans and one Brittain and two Portugall Barks all a fishing and so we made ready to depart towards Cape de Bas that is 25 leagues as shortly as we have fished and so along the coast until we may meete with our fellowe and so with all diligence that lyes in me toward parts to that Ilands that we are commanded at our departing, and that Jesu save and keep your Honourable Grace and all your Honourable reuer.

In the Haven of St. John the third day of August written in haste 1527, by your servant John Rut to his uttermost of his power.

Letter of William Keen Describing the Capture of St. John's by the French in 1708

Hon S'r:
December 21, 1708

About 4 this morning we were alarmed by the firing of several musquets & were within half an hours time reprized to heare the Fort was taken, without making resistance, some small time after the Fort surrender'd the Castle took the Alarm & fired two Cannon. All the inhabitants of that side[1] being sixty men were retired to the Castle. About 7 this morning two French officers came to assure the Inhabitants of quarters and took with them the most Master Inhabitants and Merchants into the Fort, where I saw Major Lloyd very heavy ey'd & a littel notice taken of him. In entering the Fort the French took three men- killed by the Inhabitants, about 5 in the Evening the Inhabitants & servants were imprison'd in store houses excepting some few that were left

1 The Southside of St. John's Harbour

in their own houses. A Fire happen'd and burnt two streets of houses, Mr. Russell was committed to the Guard in the Guard House, Mr. Wm Keen was confined with a guard in his own house, Captain Larround Denis was sent to have the Castle Surrender which was at first refused, the next day December 22'd the People gave up the Castle with their cannon charg'd, the French hoisted a white flagg and fired three guns; the People by this surrender was to have their cloaths & provisions & (to be) reinstated in their houses which was not comply'd with; the 24th St Ovide du Brouvillian comiss:r of the French forces sent four hund'rd sevnty-seven men prisoners of the church and the house of Mr. Collins allowing them for their subssistance, one pound of bread, four ounces of pork & four ounces of pease p'r diem, the Prisoners were set in ranks & counted by the Indians , who threatened if they found to abset themselves they would kill as many more in their roome, the 25th the French were examining the Master Inhabitants & others relating to the goods &c that were in the harbour and took an acc't of the same, the (20th ?) an express from St. Ovide went to Placentia by land; the ensuing was comonly in the Fort and did not much resort among the English, until their return of the Express, which was in nineteen days.

The French were looking out for the boat Shalloway &c that were in the Harbour & accordingly found two which they equipt with & one cut to pieces One of which they loaded with some of the best plunder, and put Major Lloyd, Lieut. Phillips engineer Vane and his wife with one French Officer call'd Le Chevalier Du Pen and sent them to Placentia- January 8: Mons"r St. Ovide sent an Officer with proposalls of ransoming the Schallops and fishing craft to the Inhabitants desiring their answer within twenty four hours and unless the People should ransome that he would send the prisoners Men Women and Children to Canada, affirming it was his Master's Instructions to keep Possession of the Country, the inhabitants desired some lonmger time to consider on this affaire, but could have no longer time than was fixed. The next day sai'ld One (gron?) Monsr. Pensanee passenger in a Shalloway for France to acquiant the Court of theri proceedings, after which the Inhabitants were a second time assembled in the house of Benger where the said Laround, left the People by producing the Article St. Ovide had made, the greater part whereof were refus'd b the severall alterations which were made Laround protesting before twas night, all the houses and boats in the Harbour, should be in flames, the Inhabitants fearing these threats, some consented to the Ransoming that night and the next day it was concluded upon; the Article was in French & English, were sign'ed by both partys, soon after returned their Express from Placentia as also one sloop with about forty men & in some few days arriv'd the Venus a shippe of twenty guns & two hundred & fifty men, two small sloops in order to load their plunder, some men were taken out of the shipp to keep in the Fort, severall boats were cut up for Fire wood & many more burnt by the French, with Store housewe which were not ransom'd; a party of men were sent from this place in Order to take Ferryland comman'd by Larond, but had no success, the People resolving not to give away the Island nor would they admitt of a flag of truce, the Inhabitants cut up their boats for to hinder any landing.

Upon Laround's return St. Ovide resolved himself to take it at the head of his Men and made as sure of it as he did of St. John's, the People belonging to the shipps were getting the bulk of their goods on board their vessel & dismounting their cannon at the Fort getting every thing in order for their departure, the Ice coming hinder'd them very much and detain'd them was a month longer than was expected, the houses in the New Fort with some few necessarys in them, some few days after the Fort was demolished and St. Ovide removed to the Castle, Mr. Lartieu one of the officers was there blown up with powder, St. Ovide & severall others had escaoped the danger there being in the next roome wass 20 quintals of powder in order to blow up the castle and demolish it, which like to have taken fire; March 27th St. Ovide sent for some of the Principal Inhabitants, and told them they must prepare to go with them to Placentia, to give his Master an accn't of what he has done so the Inhabitants here, & he promised upon his word and honour he would return them in 15 or 20 days time at the farthest, and took on board Mr Rich'd Cole, Mr. Alyn-Southmayd, Mr. Wm Keen, Mr. Thomas Russell and Mr. Wm Nicholas and sail'd out of the harbour of St. John's, the wind not being faire put back into the Harbour and took on board Mr. Collins & Mr. Squarry and carried to Placentia, the 5th April the Venus remain'd and Sloop were below Ferryland, the English Prisoners on board Venus, remain'd on board two days, after her arrival, the 3rd day went for before the governour, severall questions asked relating to the of the English by St. Ovide after examination were sent to seperate houses to live upon their own expenses, when the time was expired that St. Ovide had given his word and hgonour for their return of the Prisoners he was ask'd leave by the Prisoners to be sent home his answer tarry patiently four days more, and you shall be sent away after that four days four days more, untill the Governour assembled together three of his Officers, and made us sign to ratify and confirme the Ransomes w'th his promise that the Prisoners then in custody should be sent to St. John's in a short time; May 5th consultations was call'd relating to the English Prisoners, and it was concluded as heard, that all the Prisoners belonging to St. John's of her Maj'ts Garrison should be sent to Canada, the 10 a messenger from the Grand Seigneur to order on board the Venus, Mr. Russel, Mr. Wm Keen, Mr. Alyn- Southmayd, Mr. Ric'd Cole, Mr. John Collins digori Heart, Jno Gross, Wm. Squarry, Rick'd bowden, Jno Elliot there to be kept close prisoners and not permitted to speak to any person whatsoever, not to have the liberty to walk the Dock without a Centinal the 13th a small shipp & one Sloop with the English Prisoners on board for Canada among whom was Mr. Lloyd & Mr. Phillips, as were obtained on board close prisoners until the 18th of May & had nothing allowed us for our subsistance and had only liberty for one day to go ashore to buy our provisions, the 18th the Governour went for the English Prisoners on shaore, & told them he had a design to enlarge our liberty upon giving our Word and Honour that we would not depart without leave, which we gave him, and were returned to the great beach, excepting four that were sent to the redoubt proslners, some few days after was sent to St. John's on La Vallier with one French and two Indians, by whome the Governour gave laws and liberty to write to St. John's upon delivering the latter with his perusall & promised the prisoners that in a few days they should be set at liberty; ye 26th arriv'd the Fidel man of warr from France fifty four guns, in which shipps came over two hundred soldiers which were designed for reinforcing St. John's Forts expecting the French had not quitted it the Gov't that was sent by St. Ovide with an express to copurt returne'd in the Fidel & St. Ovide received news of his being created Knight of the Military Order of St. Lewis & Governour of St. John's/ June 2nd arrived the Galliard from Port Lewis belonging to the King and hired by merchants two hundred men who design'd to cruize on the Coast of New England; the 4th arrived La Vallier from St. John's, and inform'd the Governour that if our fleet was not arrived that there were two galleys that cruiz'ed off, to discover the arrival of our Fleet, that the said galleys had been at Bay Bulls for intelligence to direct our forces that were expected there, wee embarked in a small Ketch bought by the Prisoners, with the Grand Seigneur's leave for St. John's and arrived the 26th of June, at my departure thence, were arriv'd forty three sail of shipps, twelve from ten to twenty guns each, their Fort is very much out of repair, and a great number of men daily employ'd at work in rapaire of the same, they have double palisad'd the Westernside and mounted several guns against the entrance the Fort is only built with palidases and fill'd up with dirt without any manner of Ditch, the Fort has in it mounted upwards of fourty guns, the Redoubt upon the Hill which looks down into the Fort, path now in it about sixteen guns; of which were carried from St. John's the Redout Palisad'd round, and some small coverts built with palisades for defence of their passages to the water, at the foot of the Hill on the Larboard side coming in upon entrance between Joint Vords (Point Verde) & Crows Cuies is a small battery of Tonn guns, and about a quartr of a mile from that less another small of six gunns, all their forced lying on the Larboard side aforesaid at the narrow entrance of the Harbour is not fix'd two small chains and new cable, the Chaines link about 4 inches diameter, laid slanting by reason of the prodigious.

honourable Sr:

You have herewith the papers I promised to send you, being what remarks I could make while in the Enemy's hands.

St. John's I am
July 5, 1709
Your Hon most humble S't W. Keen

St. John's Newfoundland 16 November, 1743

My Lord:

Since my last of the 25th of September, I have employ'd all the Artificers, and Labourers I could possibly procure in restoring Fort William, and making a communication between the same and George's Battery, and have the satisfaction to acquaint your Grace, that it is already, in the condition expressed by the enclosed Plan and Profile, and to defend the same, I have left all the ordnance Scores, that could be spared from His Majesty's Ship under my command and have put therein a Captain, two lieutenants and eighty five effective Marines, which belonged to His Majesty's Ships under my command, and as Labourers were necessary, to carry on the work, I have made an agreement, with eighty English Protestants Fishermen, at eighteenth pence p(er) diem, to remain here the winter, both to carry on the works, and to assist in defending the place, in case of need, the said Fishermen to be discharged, the beginning of the Fishery in the Spring, and I have in order to make the said eighteen pence p(er) diem of the more value to them, contracted with Messrs Masters and Ballard merchants in this place, co furnish them with Provisions at eight pence p(er) deim in quantity agreeable, to what His Majesty's allowance is on board his Ships, the said eight pence to be Deducted, out of the above eighteenth pence p(er) diem.

And as the Marines were victualed on board His Majesty's ships, and all kinds of provisions being excessively dear in this Country, I thought as I left them here for His Majesty's Service, it would be cruel not to give them the same Encouragement they had when they were on ship board, Have therefore contracted with the said Messrs Masters and Ballard to victual them in the same manner as the said English Fishermen, and to enable the Contractors, to lay in Sufficient quanity of Provisions to victual the said men; I have paid them seven hundred pounds in advance.

Thomas Smith

The "Stick A Pin Here" Letter of 1835

On May 28, 1835, Robert J. Parsons, editor of the *Patriot* newspaper, was sentenced to three months imprisonment in the common jail or pay a fine of fifty pounds to the King, by Judge Bolton. Parsons's offence was that he refused to disclose the name of the author of a letter published in the *Patriot* on May 17, 1835 and signed only "Stick a Pin Here." The letter reflected on the judicial honesty of Judge Bolton. The fine was quickly collected and paid by Parsons's supporters, and he spent only a few days in jail.

St. John's
May 17, 1835

Editor of the Patriot:

We understand that a lecture was delivered in the Court-house yesterday to the Grand and Petit Juries on the opening of of the Central Court Circuit by the President of the Council in his capacity as Chief Judge on the very great benefits that hanging the people confers on society, arising no doubt from its sedative effects upon the human system, which to the uninitiated are truly astonishing. The same excellent plan is to be followed up, in order to quell the firey spirits which at this moment keep us a wholesail ripple on the surface of society, which it would appear fearfully disturbs the repose of the honourable lecturer and all other despots who shall dare to subvert the charters of the land and plant in their stead, the unalloyed principles of arbitrary sway! Go It Ye Cripples?

(Signed) Stick a Pin Here

Alexander Graham Bell's Letter

On September 2, 1885, Alexander Graham Bell, his wife Mable, his two sons, and his father were shipwrecked when the SS *Hanoverian* ran ashore at Portugal Cove South on the Southern Shore. On September 3, they came to St. John's, and shortly before their departure on the SS *Polynesian* on September 4, Alexander Graham Bell wrote a letter to the editor of the *Evening Mercury*, thanking the people of St. John's for their kindness and generosity:

St. John's,
September 8, 1885
Sir:

The appeal to the inhabitants of St. John's for aid for the steerage passengers of the *Hanoverian* has been most liberally responded to by donations of clothing and money.

As many of these donations were addressed to my care, I feel that the duty deloves upon me of thanking the donors for their generosity - which I do most heartily - and of explaining the manner in which the gifts have been applied.

A number of ladies of St. John's kindly volunteered to act as a committee to investigate the needs of the various passengers, and to distribute the clothing and money as required. The self-denying and arduous efforts of these ladies have happily been successful in accomplishing the relief of all ascertained cases of distress. The proprietor of the "Atlantic Hotel" promptly granted the committee the use of one of the rooms in his hotel; and Mr. Fred Smith, of St. John's undertook the collection and care of cash contributions - which amounted to upwards of 40 pounds.

I am sure that the unfortunate passengers of the *Hanoverian* will ever remember with gratitude the timely aid that has so cordially been extended to them.

The generosity of the people of St. John's has been so great that there will probably be a surplus which will be available for the poor of this city.

Yours truly,
Alexander Graham Bell

Appendix E

Persons willing to subscribe to the first edition of the Royal Gazette and Newfoundland Advertiser September 6, 1806—the first edition of the paper was published on August 27, 1806

Thos. Tremblett, John Harris, John Rennell, George Thesiger, A. H. Brooking, H. Phillips, Dan Coughlan, John Broom, R. Hutton, George and Thoms Keough, John Murray, Thomas Forth Winter, Alex Miller, Hunt, Epps & Gaden, William Elmer, Thos. Williams, D. Rennie, Nich. & Jos. Gill, John Ryan for George Elliot, Hunter & Company, Alex. Boucher, Thomas Meagher, Hunt, Stabb, Preston & Company, R. Pike, W. Skerrett, Thomas Cook, James O'Donel for Dr. Lambert, John Houston, William B. Rowe, Alex Haines, William Haley, W. Tonge, J. Macbriare, James Melledge, Parker & Knight, Pat Hines, D. Duggan, Dan Codner & Co., Crawford, Robertson & Co., Patton, Baine & Co., Luke Maddock, Tim Ryan, Wm. Goff, J. Williams, Henry Shea, J. Ryan for W. Newman, Eighard Langley, Walter MacAllister, John Dowsley, Augustus Mainson, Jer. Hearn, John Masters, John Stentaford, John & Peter O'Riordan, John Bonver, George Winter, Adecombe G. Henley, Cornelius Quick, Philip Breenlen, Robert Parsons, William B. Thomas, Henry Batten, John Way, Richard Cooke, Wm. Notting, Lionel Chancey, Joseph Krornagh, Wm. Best, John Barnes, Simon Solomon, Peter Lemessurier, Dan Marett & Co., John Barry, Wm. Walsh, Tim Flannery, John P. Grace, John Scott, Charles Hutchings, David Brien, B. Johnson, John Travers, Peter McAusian, Geo. Lilly, John Snelgrove, Joseph Costello, James June, Joseph Whiteway, Samuel Prowse, R. E. Armstrong, Francis Hanlain, Thos. G. Mackim, Richard King, R. Tuffe for Wm. Armstrong, Dominie King, John Wall, Goss & Butler per L. Knight, Bombardier Lindas, Wm. Noble,

David Dodrick, Philip Christian, Capt. Muddle, James Anderson, John Murch, Anthony Steward, Alex Hutchinson, Sergt. J. P. Klein, Sergt. Alex McLeod,, James Strikley, Robert Hanmmill, Mr. Parker, Mr. Linagar, Capt. Summerville, Dr. Thompson, George Trapnell, Thomas Murphy, J. Biggs, Dr. Trembell, Peter Mvkie, His Excellency John Holloway, Esq., John Villeneufue & Co., John Dunn, Mr. Langley, Wm. Power, Miller & Fergus, Arnall, Dalton & Arnall, Dinah Elliot, G. Kemble & Co., James Kennedy, John Tanner, John Haley, Mrs. Geo. Best, ry Parsons, Dr. Dunnogan, Wm. Denning, Dr. Connors, Dr. Shea, Dr. Dan O'Connor, Richard Shea, Joseph Tumbaum, Wm. Pinsent, Thomas Mullowney, Mr. Langley, Wm. J. Delaney, Thomas Ever, Dr. Sterling, Richard Kelan, Mrs. Maloney, J. Churchill & Co., James Brown, James Cawley, Samuel Newman, David Dunell, Joseph Glover, Wm. Taylor, James Lane, John and R. Brien, Thomas Atkens, Richard Langley, Archibald Nevins, Richard Hammond, Thomas Murphy, Robert Dooling, Michael Murphy, Wm. Branscombe, John Harvey, Wm. Phipard, Pat Murrin for Wm. Power, M. Farrell, John Brophy, Robert Lee, George Hutchings, John Winter, M. Warren, W. Boden, W. Withycombe, W. Rendell, Jr., John Williams, Wm. Stephenson, Murphy & Gleeson, John Burke, Walter Murphy, Follett, Hoyles & Co., Edward Kenny, John Godfrey, Lieut. Estaff, Wm. MacLeod, W. Warren, T. A. Ruggles, Francis Gilman, (N.S.R. Quartermaster), F. Goff, John Steward, Wm. Kirby, Ben Johnson, Joseph Church, John Byrne, Rich. Purcell, R. A., Alex. Dunbsten, Rover Angel, Mrs. Withycombe, M. Neave & Sons, James Sinyard, John Keith, John Shuett, Michael Currun, Pat Murrin, Charlew Jade, R. Keefe, Arch. C. Dodd, Esq., Richard Hooper, Mr. Solomon, Constable Phippard, Sergt. Grant, Mr. Street, Sergt. James Brophy, John Duncanson, Sergt. John Congdon, Mr. Byrne, Mrs. King, Adjt. Moores, Mr. McCarthy, Sergt. Dent, Jacob Habs, Mr. Roe, Sergt. McCullach, Matthew Henesey, W. P. Carter, Sergt. John Brady, George Gutheridge, Sergt. Stewart Williamson, M. D., Wm. Matthews, Stuart S. Hill, Rev. Parson Vialette, Sergt. James Brophy, Mr. Warren, Stephen Woolcock, Jonathan Parsons, Mich. Curran, Mr. John Wall, Thomas Dolenty & Co., Gosse, Chancey & Co., A. Nevins, Roberts and Moore, James O'Donald, Michael Hennessey,

Robert Kenny, James Brown, R. A., Levi MulCulloch, Parsons & Glover, Dr. James Oakley, Mrs. Towill, N. Gibbs, Lieut. J. McNab, John Guest, Wm. Raystone, Thomas Parr, Esq., Mrs. Lily Kearney & St. John, Alexander Camel, M. O'Lannigan, Wm. Lily, Jordan & Henderson, Wm. Jordan, Thomas Parsons, Wm. Adams, Philip Coats, Wm. Brien, H. E. Gaden, Wm. Cull, Mr. Hampton, George Moulton, Peter Brown, Richard Bishop, Rev. A. Fitzpatrick, Dr. Nicholas Brand, Mrs. Butler, Mr. McCarimon, Mr. Canada, Wm. Barnes.

Appendix F

In 1815, the British Admiralty issued a "Protection" against impressment for the crew and passengers of the ship Liven, bound from London to St. John's, Newfoundland. A short description of the crew and passengers was attached to the "Protection"

Name	**Age**	**Height Ft.**	**In**	**Complexion**
			Crew	
Smith William	21	5	5	Fair, grey eyes, Dk brown hair
Winks William	27	5	5	Fair, short, sandy hair
Taylor John	21	5	5	Sallow, short, brown hair
Taylor Thomas	27	5	9	Fair, short, brown hair
Heath Richard	19	5	4	Fair, short, light sandy hair
Mortimer James	23	5	6	Dark, short, black hair
Williams Will	20	5	4	Swarthy, short, sandy hair, Lame in right leg
			Passengers	
Baggs Henry	24	5	8	Dark, dark grey eyes
Bearns Robert	42	5	4	Dark, marvel eyes, black hair
Blake Richard	25	5	3	Swarthy, short, sandy hair
Boon William	25	5	6	Brown, short, dark hair
Bradey James	23	5	4	Brown, one eye, dark hair
Bright John	25	5	9	Brown, grey eyes, brown hair
Brown Richard	19	5	8	Dark, full face, hazel eyes Dark brown hair, cut on hand

Burgoin John	27	5	11	Little, pitted with small pox, Blue eyes, dark brown hair
Clarke William	30	5	2	Dark, dark eyes and hair
Collins Nick	22	5	7	Fair, grey eyes, brown hair
Cooke Stephen	56	5	7	Fair, short, brown hair
Coonan William	21	5	4	Dark, short, black hair
Crud William	14	4	2	Sallow, short, light hair
Davie Richard	22	5	9	Dark, black eyes, black hair Long face
Diment Tom	21	5	8	Fair, hazel eyes, light hair
Dowing John	25	5	7	Dark, long face, brown hair
Edwards Tom	26	5	2	Brown, dark grey eyes, Black hair
Elliott James	25	5	6	Fair, short, sandy hair
Farrier James	43	5	5	Fair, short, light hair
Grant Stephen	41	5	8	Fair, grey eyes, brown hair
Groot John	25	6	0	Brown, dark hair
Harvey William	23	5	2	Ruddy, short, dark hair
Hooper Tom	35	5	5	Brown, hazel eyes
Howe Will	19	5	5	Fair, hazel eyes, black hair, Cut on right side of face
Inkpen Michael	47	5	5	Ruddy, grey eyes, brown hair Tinged with grey
Kennelly Will	29	5	10	Dark, black eyes and hair
Langdon Elias	17	5	7	Sallow, short, sandy hair
Lay William	25	5	5	Fair, hazel eyes, brown hair
Luscombe Rich	24	5	8	Ruddy, brown hair
Mitchell George	26	5	7	Fair, short, sandy hair
Mitchell Nick	22	5	7	Ruddy, grey eyes, brown hair
Mitchell Will	25	5	6	Ruddy, grey eyes, brown hair
Mundy Henry	21	5	4	Dark, dark brown hair
Newell George	22	5	7	Fair, dark brown hair
Peters William	47	5	5	Pale, black hair
Phillips Peter	20	5	6	Red face, grey eyes, dark Brown hair
Pierce John	43	5	3	Sallow, short, dark hair
Pierce Richard	23	5	9	Pale, hazel eyes, brown hair
Pope John	23	5	11	Fair, short, brown hair
Pope Langley	19	5	10	Fair, short, brown hair
Roper John	23	5	7	Ruddy, grey eyes, dark hair

Sampson Tom	26	5	5	Grey eyes, brown hair, Marked with small pox
Sanford James	23	5	4	Fair, black eyes, dark hair
Shears Steve	19	5	8	Brown, grey eyes, dark hair
Steer Henry	21	5	6	Brown, grey eyes, brown hair
Suffel John	16	4	8	Fair, grey eyes, light hair, Rather long face
Trood John	44	5	8	Fair, grey eyes, black hair, Scar on right hand
Trust Nick	28	5	7	Brown, hazel eyes, full face
Tucker Joseph	22	5	8	Dark brown, grey eyes, Dark hair
Vinning Henry	17	5	5	Fair, black eyes
Wadden Will	38	5	7	Fair, short, dark hair
Wills Henry	28	5	5	Light, brown hair, grey eyes
Wills James	17	4	11	Ruddy, grey eyes, Light brown hair, knee knocked
Wicks William	21	5	3	Fair, grey eyes, dark hair
Windsor John	45	6	0	Brown, grey eyes, dark hair
Windsor Samuel	44	5	3	Dark, grey eyes, black hair

Bibliography

Anspach, Rev. Louis, *A History of Newfoundland*, London, 1827.

Baker, Melvin, *Aspects of 19th Century St. John's,* 1982.

Birkenhead, Lord, *The Story of Newfoundland,* London, 1920.

Bonneycastle, Sir Richard, *Newfoundland in 1842*, London, 1842.

Byrne, Cyril J., *Gentlemen-Bishops and Faction Fighters*, St. John's, 1984.

Byrnes, John M., *The Paths To Yesterday*, Boston, 1931.

Devine, P. K., *Ye Olde St. John's*, 1936.

Devine & O'Mara, *Notable Events in the History of Newfoundland,* St. John's, 1900.

Cell, Gillian T., *English Enterprise in Newfoundland 1577 -1680,* Toronto, 1969.

Benevolent Irish Society, Centenary Volume, St. John's, 1906.

Chappell, Lieut. Edward, *Voyage of His Majesty's Ship Rosamond to Newfoundland*, London, 1818.

English, L. E. F., *Historic Newfoundland,* Montreal, 1967.

Fay, C. R., *Life and Labour in Newfoundland,* Cambridge, 1956.

Gunn, Gertrude, *The Political History of Newfoundland 1832-1864* Toronto, 1966.

Harvey, Rev. M., *A Short History of Newfoundland*, London, 1890.

Harvey, M. Hatton J., *Newfoundland*, London, 1883.

Head, Grant, *Eighteenth Century Newfoundland*, Toronto, 1976.

Hibbs, R., *The Newfoundland Road Booster*, St. John's, 1924.

Howley, James, *The Beothucks or Red Indians*, Cambridge, 1915.

Howley, Rt. Rev., *Ecclesiastical History of Newfoundland*, Boston, 1888.

Innis, Harold, *The Cod Fishery,* Toronto, 1954.

Jukes, J. B., *Excursions In and About Newfoundland* (2 Vol) London, 1842.

Keir, David, *The Bowring Story,* London, 1962.

Lounsbury, Ralph, *The British Fishery in Newfoundland*, 1634-1763 (Reprint Ed.) Hamden, 1969.

McCrea, Robert, *Lost Amid the Fogs*, London, 1869.

McGrath, P. T. *Newfoundland in 1911*, London, 1911.

Moyles, R. G., *Complaints is many and Various, but the odd Divil likes it*, Toronto, 1975.

Mosdell, H. M., *When was That?*, St. John's, 1922.

Murphy, James, *The Colony of Newfoundland*, St. John's, 1925.
Customs of the Past, St. John, 1918.

Murphy, Michael, *Pathways Through Yesterday*, St. John's, 1976.

Murray, Jean, *The Newfoundland Journal of Aaron Thomas,* Don Mills, 1968.

O'Neill, Paul, *The Oldest City*, Erin, Ontario, 1975.
A Seaport Legacy, Erin, Ontario, 1976.

Pedley, Rev. Charles, *The History of Newfoundland,* London, 1863.

Perlin, A. B., *The Story of Newfoundland*, St. John's, 1959.

Prowse, D. W., *A History of Newfoundland*, London, 1895.

Reeves, John, *A History of the Government of the Island of Newfoundland*, London, 1793.

Rodgers, J. D., *A Historical Geography of Newfoundland,* Vol. V, Oxford, 1911.

Rowe, Frederick W., *Education and Culture in Newfoundland,* Toronto, 1976.

Smallwood, J. R., *The Books of Newfoundland*, (6 volumes) St. John's, 1967.

Smallwood, J. R. etc. *The Encyclopedia of Newfoundland*, (5 volumes) St. John's, 1981-1994.

Smith, Harry J., *Newfoundland Holiday,* Toronto, 1952.

Toque, Rev. Philip, *Newfoundland as It Is In 1877*, Toronto, 1878.

Webber, David, *Skinner's Fencibles*, St. John's, 1964.

- Newspaper Articles -

Christmas Bells, St. John's, 1897, 1899, 1900, 1909.

Christmas Chimes, St. John's, December 1911, 1913.

Christmas Review, St. John's, 1892.

Courier, May 11, 1872.

Evening Chronicle, St. John's, December 27, 1911.

Evening Herald, July 9, 1891.

Royal Gazette, St. John's, November 11, 1822, August 15, 1837.

The Newfoundlander, December 2, 1861, June 20, 1843.

St. John's Evening Telegram, July 2, 1909, June 7, 1909, November 7, 1896, July 3, 1933, April 20, 1967.

St. John's Daily News, July 3, 1935, July 5, 1933.

Senior News, St. John's, January 19, 1989.

Times, St. John's, December 12, 1855, July 26, 1856.

- Other Government and Private Documents -

Alberti Papers, C.O. 195/2.

Calendar of State Papers, 1675.

Colonial Papers Vols. XXII, XXXV, XXXVIII.

Colonial Letterbooks, 1749-1831.

C.O. 194/3,f, 194/7, 194/25, 194/37, C.O. 194/38, 194/42.
C.O.195/13, C.O. 196/13.

Newman Hunt Records 1798-1806, Nfld. Archives.

St. John's Harbour & Pilotage Commission, July 31, 1933, p. 93

Index

Adams, William G., 141-144, 166, 167, 199
Airport Heights, 33, 145
Anglican Cathedral, 17, 18, 76
Anspach, Lewis Amadeus, 20
Arts and Culture Centre, 21, 33
Athenaeum, 21, 180
Avalon Course, 15

Bannerman, Alexander, 29
Bannerman Park, 29, 78
Baron Morris of Waterford, 14
Basilica, 13, 14, 18, 131, 179, 183, 185, 187
Bay Bulls, 9, 192
Bell Chute, 27
Belvedere Orphanage, 112
Benevolent Irish Society, 13, 20, 68, 180
Bennett's Grove, 111
Beothuk women, 23, 24
Berry, John, 5
Bevill, Mildred, 44-47
Bingwell, Samuel, 121-124
Bishop Feild College, 20
Bishop, Joseph, 99
Bishop's College, 20
Bishop Spencer College, 20
Blackhead, 51-54, 175, 177
Blundon, William, 92, 94
Bond, Robert, 128, 129, 132
Booth Memorial, 20
Bowdin, Caroline, 29
Bowring Brothers, 30, 72, 89, 97, 103, 132, 138
Bowring Park, 29, 30, 112, 131, 135, 140
Bowring Park Committee, 138
Bradstreet, John, 43
Bray's Well, 27
Brother Rice, 20
Buckmaster's Field, 32, 141, 143
Bunker, Elizabeth, 40, 41
Bunker, Richard, 40
Burke, Johnny, 29
Bute, Captain, 119-121

Cabot Celebrations, 146
HMS *Calypso*, 109
Campbell, Colin, 40
Canada Summer Games, 144
Canadian Forces in St. John's, 32
Cantwell, James, 88-92, 177
Capital Coach Lines, 140
Captain Kidd, 111
Carbonear Island, 8
card games, 15
Carnell, Andrew Greene, 134, 136-140, 162-164
Carnell, John, 128, 155, 156
Carroll's Well, 27
Carter, Walter Carmichel, 150, 166, 167
Cartier, Jacques, 3
Chafe Nursing Home fire, 1976, 81
Chain Rock, 92, 95, 114, 177
Chappell, Edward, 16
Christine, 39-41, 44
Church of England chapel, 17
Circular Road, 111
Civic Centre/Convention Centre Complex, 141, 151
Civic Relief Committee, 136
Coffee, Philip, 42-44
Coffin, Ann, 44-47
Coffin, John, 44, 46
Collins, Captain, 87
Colonial Building, 22, 25, 26
colourful St. John's characters, 29

Commission of Government, 25, 32, 131, 137
Confederation, 33, 129, 140, 185
Confederation Building, 25
Connel, Catharine, 59, 60
Cook, Tasker, 134-136, 161
Corsair, 98
Cox, Daniel, 45
Crowe, Josias, 6, 38, 187
Cuckhold's Cove Head, 96
Cuckhold's Cove wreck, 95-98
Cull, William, 23, 199

Deadman's Pond, 111
Delight, 86, 87
DeLisle, Captain, 92
Demasduit, 23
de Ruyter, 5
de Sance, Michel, 4
Desola, 110
Dinn, Jerome W., 150
Dr. Hunter Library, 21
Dooley, Dennis, 62
Doyle, Richard, 46
duel of March 30, 1826, 61, 62
duel of September 25, 1873, 62, 63
Duff, Suzanne, 142, 146, 148, 149, 169-171, 173, 174
Duke of Connaught, 30
Dunfield, Brian E. S., 137

earthquake report, 30, 184
Ellis, William J., 130-132, 157-159
Enos, Captain, 98, 99

Ferryland, 8, 129, 131, 191
Fever Hospital, 22
Fielding, William, 42-44
fire at Riverhead, 72, 73, 75
fire of 1855, 27, 74
fire of 1856, 74, 75
fire of December 21, 1708, 67
fire of November 21, 1817, 70-72
fires of 1816, 18, 67, 68, 71
fires of 1833, 1839, 1840, and 1846, 72-74, 127
fire of November 7, 1817, 68-72
first Baptist church, 19
first Congregational church, 19
first election, 128, 155
first grammar school, 20
first hospital, 22
first House of Assembly, 24
first official census, 5, 6
first Pentecostal church, 19
first Roman Catholic church, 18
first library, 21, 180
first Salvation Army temple, 19
first Seventh-Day Adventist church, 19
first synagogue, 19
first water from Windsor Lake, 27, 184
first woman mayor, 143-145
Flaherty's First Fire, 75
Flower Hill, 15
Foran Hotel, 116-119
Forrester, James, 57
Fort Amherst, 85, 102, 103
Fort Pepperrell, 32
Fort Townshend, 8, 22, 23
Fort Townshend Hollow, 62, 63
Fort William, 7, 17, 37, 85, 193
Freeman, Samuel, 45
French attacks on St. John's, 7-9, 67, 189-193
Friendly Hall, 111
Fry, John, 39

Garden, 4
Gardner, George, 55-58
Garrett's Well, 27
Garrison Hill Well, 27
Geisha, 98, 99, 176
General Hospital, 22, 94
George's Pond, 27
ghost of Casey's Lane, 112-116
ghost of Long Pond Road, 119-121
ghosts and haunted places, 109-124
Gibbet Hill, 55
Gibbs, Michael P., 129-131, 158
Gibsone, John, 7
Gilbert, Humphrey, 3, 4, 86, 146
Gilmore, Margaret, 55-58

Gilmore, William, 55-58
Gonzaga High School, 20, 112
Gosling Memorial Library, 21, 179
Gosling, William Gilbert, 130, 132, 133, 159, 160
Goulds, 33, 81, 149, 171
Government House, 8, 22, 29, 73, 183
Gower, Erasmus, 24
Gower Street church, 18, 76
Grace Hospital, 22
Grand Battery, 8
Grant, Colonel, 26
Great Fire of 1892, 17, 19, 75-79, 82, 110, 117, 127

Halleran, Matthew, 52-55
Hamilton, Charles, 71
Handside, Thomas, 8
Harrington, Michael, 140
Harris, Jack, 150
Harvey, John, 72, 73
Harvey Road, 13, 19, 79, 82, 187
Harvey Road fire, 1992, 82
Hayes, Edward, 86
Hayes, Mick, 55-58
Healey, Gus, 62, 63
Health Sciences Complex, 22, 23
Henley, Alec G., 143, 166
Henry Street, 18, 75
Henry Street fire of 1859, 75
Hermit, 28
Holy Cross School, 20
Holy Heart High School, 20
Howlett, Charles J., 134, 136, 162
Hull House fire of 1948, 80, 81

incorporation of St. John's, 25
Ingraham, 101
Irish Christian Brothers, 20, 180
Irish immigrants, 11, 12, 14, 68

Jackson, John, 37, 39
Jackson, Margaret, 39, 40
Janeway Children's Hospital, 23
Jehovah's Witnesses, 19
Jensen, Hans, 96, 98
Jessie B, 99
John Casey's barn, 62, 63

Keats, Richard Goodwin, 17
Keef, Catherine, 55-58
Keene's meadow, 42
Keen's wharf, 55
Keen, William, 10, 51-55, 67, 189-193
Keen, William Jr., 53
Kelly, P. W., 128
Kelly, W. A. O'D, 133
Keough Estate Building, 128
Kilbride, 33, 145
King Henry VIII, 3, 188
King, John, 141
Kirke, David, 5
Kirk, 19, 187
Kitchin, William, 59
Knights of Columbus Hostel fire, 1942, 79, 80, 82
Knowlan, Patrick, 60

Lady James Pearl, 112
Lambly, Lawrence, 52-55
Langman, Edward, 12
le Magor, Philip, 123, 124
Lester's Field, 32
lighthouse at Cape Spear, 85, 88, 91, 101
Lloyd, Thomas, 37-39, 41, 189, 190, 192
Lloyd, William Frederick, 132
local militia, 10
London Tavern, 13, 16, 17, 180
Long Bridge, 22, 135
Longshoremen's Protective Union, 129

MacCormac, Picton R., 137
Maggie, 92-95, 176
Mainwaring, Henry, 4
March, Mary, 23
Marconi, Guglielmo, 30, 187
Marshall, Susanna, 40, 41
SS *Marsland*, 102-105, 177
Martin, Cabot J., 151
Martin, William, 96, 98
McAusland, 27
McDonald, Paul, 52-55

McGuire, Edmund, 52-55
McNicholas, Patrick, 144
Medical Society formed, 28
Melville, Elizabeth, 42-44
Memorial University College, 30
Methodist College, 20
Mews, Henry George Reginald, 134, 139-141, 164-166
Monroe, Moses, 128, 155
Moody, John, 39-41
Moore, Ann, 42-44
Morris, Edward Patrick, 14, 132
Morris, Isaac Chesley, 133, 135, 159, 160
Morrison, William, 128
Mount Cashel, 20
Mount Pearl, 15, 33, 141, 151
Mullock Street, 111
Municipal Act (51 Vic., C.5), 127, 128
Munn, Thomas, 46
Murphy, John Joseph, 142, 144-146, 149, 168-170, 172
Murphy, Robert, 141

new City Hall, 141
Newfoundland Historic Trust, 146
Newfoundland School Society, 20
New Gower Street, 78, 80, 81, 116, 136, 141
new military hospital, 22

O'Brien, Smith, 14, 180
O'Donel, James Louis, 13, 18, 183, 197
Old Chapel, 18
old St. Mary's Anglican Church, 24, 28
Oliver, Richard, 40
O'Neill, Raymond Andrew, 145, 168-172
Osborne, Henry, 10, 11

Palk's Farm, 22
Palliser, Hugh, 12
Payne, W., 4
Peyton, John, 23
Philpot, John, 61, 62, 111
Phoebe, 102, 177
Pickmore, Francis, 67-71, 187
Pilot's Cove, 102
Pleasantville, 23, 32
Power, Eleanor, 51-55
Power, Margeret, 58, 59
Power, Mary, 59, 60
Power, Michael, 128, 155, 156
Power, Robert, 51-55
Presentation Sisters, 20
Prim, Peter, 60
Prince Henry of the Netherlands, 88, 92
Prince of Wales College, 20, 150
Prince Philip Drive, 146

Queen's Road, 19, 78, 111
Quidi Vidi Lake, 21, 32, 121-124, 145
Quidi Vidi murder of 1754, 51-55

Reid Newfoundland Company, 129
Rennie's Bridge, 61, 11, 135
Rennie's Mill River, 27
Republic of Newfoundland, 12, 13
Responsible Government, 25, 32, 33, 137
Ridley, Margaret, 44-46
Roberval, 3
Roman Catholic Cathedral, 13, 18, 27, 78, 179, 183, 185, 187
Rotary Club, 22, 145, 187
Royal Newfoundland Constabulary, 11
Rudkin, Mark, 61-63
Rut, John, 3, 188, 189
Ryan, Michael, 43, 44

St. Andrew's Society, 24
St. Bonaventure's College, 20
St. Bride's College, 20
St. Clare's Hospital, 22, 112
St. John, Francis, 128, 155
St. John's Fire Companies, 11
St. John's Fire Department, 11
St. John's Heritage Foundation, 146
St. John's Housing Corporation, 140
St. John's Regatta, 21
St. John's Transportation Commission, 140

St. Ovide, 8, 190-192
St. Patrick's Church, 13, 112, 131, 180
St. Patrick's Hall School, 20, 27, 76, 78
Salem, Massachusetts, 123, 124
Salmah, 89-92, 177
Seaman's Home, 131, 158
Shawnadithit, 23, 24
Shea, George Edward, 77, 129, 130, 147, 157
Shea Heights, 33, 145
Shea, Ambrose, 77, 106, 129, 184
Shea, Katherine, 58, 59
Short, Mrs., 37, 38
Sick Bay Number 6, 22
Signal Hill, 9, 27, 30, 78, 85, 103, 111, 187
Sisters of Mercy, 20, 22
Smith, Flipper, 29
Snow, Catherine, 111
Souris Bell, 99-101, 178
Southern Cross, 109, 110
South Head, 85, 175
Southlands, 33, 151
Southmead, 10
Southside Castle, 8
Southside Hill fire of August 14, 1876, 75, 177
HMS *Sphynx*, 121, 122, 124
Spratt, James J., 140, 163, 164
Squires, Richard Anderson, 30, 129, 133, 136
Stella, 95-98, 177
Stephens, James, 14
Straight Talk, 150
Strange, R. J., 102
streets of Olde St. John's, 27
Sunshine Camp, 22
Sutcliff, Richard, 55-58

taverns and inns in St. John's in 1807, 16, 17
third municipal election, 128
Thorburn, Robert, 127, 128
SS *Tiber*, 92-94
Tobin, Nicholas, 52-54
Tooton swimming pool, 141
Torbay, 9, 32
Town Planning Commission, 135, 162
Travers, Mary, 24, 25, 180
Trilligan, Matt, 113-116
Tucker, James Roy Wilson, 165, 166
Tybol, Kate, 56, 57
Tyllyard, John, 39-41

Vardy, Oliver Lawrence, 140, 164
Victoria Park, 22, 29, 141
Vulture, 87, 88, 178

Waterford, 12, 14
Waterford Hospital, 22
Wedgewood Park, 33, 149, 171
Wells, Andrew, 146, 148, 150-152, 169-173
Weston, Peter, 10
Wheyland, Edward, 44-46
Wheyland, Katherine, 42, 44
Whitbourne, Sir Richard, 4
Williams, David, 55-58
Winderdown, John, 39
Windsor Lake, 27, 131, 135, 143, 184
Wyatt, Dorothy, 142-145, 148, 168-174

SS *Yankton*, 110
York Street, 22

About the Authors

Frank Galgay is a prominent Newfoundland educator and author. He holds B.A. and M.Ed. degrees in classical languages and education, and has served as teacher and administrator in a number of Newfoundland schools. He is the author of *The Life and Times of Sir Ambrose Shea*, *A History of the Southern Shore* and *Everybody's Business*. He has co-authored some best-selling Newfoundland books: *Shipwrecks of Newfoundland and Labrador*, *A Christmas Box*, *Buried Treasures of Newfoundland and Labrador*, and a history of communications called *Voice of Generations*. He is married to the former Rosemary McDonald and has four children: Colleen, Sean, Brendan and Matthew. Mr. Galgay resides in St. John's and is serving a second term as a St. John's City Councillor.

Michael J. McCarthy was born in St. Jacques, Fortune Bay, moving to Terrenceville at the age of five, where he attended school until Grade XI. He attended Memorial University of Newfoundland and University of Ottawa, graduating with an M.A. degree in Literature. He taught in a number of communities until his retirement in 1986. Mike is the author of three novels: *The Journey Home*, *The Treasure of Kelly's Island* and *Escape*, together with a history of *The Irish in Newfoundland*. He has co-authored *Shipwrecks of Newfoundland and Labrador*, *The Angry Seas*, *A Christmas Box*, *Fables, Fairies and Folklore*, *Buried Treasures of Newfoundland and Labrador*, and a history of communications called *Voice of Generations*. Mr. McCarthy has also written for several magazines, as well as radio and television. He is married to the former Ann Hamlyn and has two children: Michael and Karen. He resides in Mount Pearl.